ORGANON

SPECIFIC HOMŒOPATHY;

OR,

AN INDUCTIVE EXPOSITION

OF THE

Principles of the Homoeopathic Healing Art,

ADDRESSED TO

PHYSICIANS AND INTELLIGENT LAYMEN.

BY

CHARLES J. HEMPEL, M. D.

Fellow and Corresponding Member of the Homœopathic Medical College of Pennsylvania; Honorary Member of the Hahnemann Society of London, &c. &c.

PHILADELPHIA:
PUBLISHED BY RADEMACHER & SHEEK, 239 ARCH STREET.
NEW YORK:—WILLIAM RADDE, 322 BROADWAY.
ST. LOUIS:—J. G. WESSELHŒFT, 79 MARKET STREET.
1854.

KING & BAIRD, PRINTERS, SANSOM STREET, PHILADELPHIA.

INTRODUCTION.

Two principles make up the structure of universal order. We meet them in every department of knowledge, in every form of art, either in a state of antagonism or harmony. They are variously named in the various spheres of thought and observation; duty and right, passion and reason, progress and conservatism, represent respectively the same principles in different orders of ideas. Whenever these principles are fully and freely united, a state of truth, or, at any rate, the highest approximation to truth that it is possible for finite minds to attain, is realized in that particular instance. Men's minds are constantly, although often unconsciously, gravitating toward such a union. Even those who oppose it, do so in most cases for the sake, and in the name of, what they believe to be truth. Some oppose it from motives of sordid interest, others from selfish ambition, and malicious envy or jealousy; but generally the opposition arises from ignorance of the truth, and from a blind regard for that which had been accepted as such upon the authority of others.

It is a law of human development that appearances of truth should at first be mistaken for the actual facts. Sensual perceptions constitute the first truths to the dawning intellect. In reality, all such perceptions may be as false as they seem true to the senses. They might be termed true illusions. Even the positive sciences were originally based upon sensual illusions. In astronomy it was supposed that the sun revolves round the earth, simply because he *seems* to rise in the east, and set in the west. In geography the earth was supposed to be what it actually seems, and what some Indian tribes believe it be even now, an expanse of land floating upon the waters, or fastened to the heavens by invisible chains, and touched by the clouds at the outer borders, beyond which a frightened fancy conjured up an abyss of chaotic darkness, inhabited by devouring monsters, or illumined here and there by the lurid flames of the infernal abode. Intellectual truths did not dawn upon the minds, until long after the habitual belief in sensual illusions had confirmed man in the love and defence of error. To establish the science of astronomy upon a basis of truth, its leaders had to bid defiance to the boundless powers of the Church. To substitute any actual truth in the place of a sensual illusion in any science or art, was a task that could only be accomplished by means of unwearying efforts, and a self-sacrificing devotion. In medicine likewise, all the first generalizations of the incipient science were enunciations of sensual perceptions. Because the arteries were found empty after death, it was supposed that they never contained any thing but air; hence the name artery, which has been preserved up to this day, although it embodies an essential falsehood; for its meaning is "air-containing vessel," from the Greek words (*aër*) air and *terein* (to hold or contain); and yet we know, since the magnificent discoveries of Harvey, that these vessels, so far from containing air, are, on the contrary, canals through which the blood circulates with undeviating regularity. Even in the names which have been assigned to diseases, the sensual perception of the pathological phenomena has been taken as the guiding or determining principle of nomenclature. On beholding a state of inflammatory fever, with a full and bounding pulse, we look upon this condition of the organism as one of vital exaltation, whereas, it is in reality a state of depression of the vital principle. The high arterial action exists only in appearance; the truth is that, in fever, the capillary circulation is embarrassed, obstructed in consequence of the depressed action of the capillary nerves, and that the apparent tumult or excitement in the larger arterial trunks, is simply a result of the capillary embarrassment. In the last part of this work this subject will be dwelt upon with more minuteness. So the heat and dryness of the skin in a feverish state of the system, or the pathological condition which, from time immemorial, has been termed a state of inflammation, do not, by any means, as has been generally supposed, indicate a vital turgescence; this apparent turgescence is simply an illusion of the senses, whereas, in reality, the heat and dryness of the skin arise from the fact, that the skin ceases to absorb moisture from the atmospheric air, by means of which, in a normal state of the organism, the evolution of heat in consequence of the oxydation of the tissues is counterbalanced and kept at a normal elevation; and an inflammation, together with its characteristic signs of heat, swelling, pain, and so forth, is likewise a sign of capillary depression or torpor, whereas, according to the common doctrine of pathologists, it is a result of vital expansion or sur-excitation. On examining in this manner, with the eye of reason, the actual edifice of medicine, we shall find that the existing nomenclature of pathology has a sensual origin, and that the prevailing ideas concerning the nature of disease, have likewise a sensual basis. One person is said to have too much blood, whereas this pathological condition is not, properly speaking, a condition of plethora, but of deficiency of capillary nervous action, which again may either be the mediate or immediate cause of plethora; its primary cause may be an abnormal condition of the brain, the immediate result of which might be a depression of the capillary action, and the secondary result an abnormal expansion in the sanguineous system. In another case it is said that a man has too much bile, and he is anxious to swallow an emetic for the purpose of getting rid of the bile on his stomach. He is not aware that, if the biliary system properly performed its functions of secretion, there would not be any bile on the stomach, and that, if this bile is to be removed, the removal cannot be accomplished by the mechanical operation of an emetic, but that it should be effected by restoring the secretory action of the liver to its normal condition, a mode of treatment which has as little to do with the mechanical irritation of the stomach, by means of an emetic, as the mechanical irritation of the tongue by pepper or mustard would have to do with the cure of ophthalmia.

This tendency to start in the development of science from a sensual basis, prevails in all the varied forms of intellectual life, not only in science, but likewise in art, in government, education, social institutions, in the organization of the church. It is not till the human mind has struggled long and hard, that it succeeds in divesting itself from the bondage of sensual illusions, and from the equally crushing and paralysing bondage of traditional authority; that it ceases to identify truth, be it in science, religion, or art, with the form under which it was announced by its first discoverer; and that it dares to, and finally considers it its duty and legitimate right to, penetrate and explore the realm of truth, independently of established formulas, theories or methods.

The followers of Hahnemann have exhibited the same child-like faith in the words of their master that characterises the blind and unreasoning obedience of the disciples of a religious leader to his dictates and opinions. Homœopathy was the work and property of Hahnemann, and it would have seemed as unjustifiable an outrage to alter an iota of its tenets without his consent, as it now seems to invade another man's house and alter its arrangements without the permission of the owner. Homœopathy was not a divine science that belongs exclusively to God, and which he created for our common benefit. It would seem, from the fanatical vehemence with which the most dignified, candid, and logically expressed doubts of Hahnemann's infallibility were repelled by his original followers, that homœopathy was looked upon as a thing of human ingenuity, and that its universal proportions were to be narrowed down to the limited and illusory horizon of the finite human understanding. It is probable that Hahnemann himself entertained the belief, that his discovery was all but perfect, and it is, therefore, pardonable that his disciples should have accepted his statements without discussion. This takes place whenever a new doctrine is started by a reformer, who, by his personal character, by the force and cogency of his reasoning, or by the unimpeachable evidence of facts, succeeds in making converts to his system. His followers accept his statements as infallible testimony; the words of the master are looked upon as a sacred record, and all his technicalities of style, and his peculiar modes of reasoning,—instead of being looked upon as changeable manifestations of the finite understanding,—are set down as principles which admit of no improvement, and, Minerva-like, started out of the brain of their discoverer in all the fulness of their truth and glory. This species of fanaticism is decidedly out of place in the present age; it is particularly condemnable in matters of science, and, upon a closer examination of the scientific attainments of those who indulge in it, it will be found that they constitute a set of money-making, loud-mouthed, impertinent drones, or ambitious starvelings in the world of ideas. By means of worldly tact and rhetorical cunning, they may succeed in obtaining for a season a flashy popularity in uninformed circles, but what is their unavoidable fate? Crushed by the oblivion of history and the contempt of reason, they are doomed to disappear before the memory of those bold and honest friends of science, who had dared to free the divine offspring from the fetters of human authority, and to put humanity in possession of the universal, unsullied truth.

For years past it has been my opinion, that the existing practice of homœopathy did not, by any means, realise its claims to the character of a clear, positive, and certain science; that the homœopathic Materia Medica is filled with a number of unreliable, and, therefore, useless symptoms; that a number of substances have been introduced into the Materia Medica which are not, properly speaking, drugs, and cannot, therefore, be treated as remedial agents in the common acceptation of the term; and that the high purposes of our art, and the interests of our patients require a simplification of the materials with which the homœopathic physician has been obliged to work heretofore. Homœopathic physicians who treat diseases strictly by the book, and, as they suppose, in accordance with the symptoms, use half a dozen or even a dozen medicines, where other homœopathic physicians, who have fully mastered the spirit as well as the letter of their doctrine, will achieve the same results with one or two medicines only, in much less time, and in a much more thorough, safe, and agreeable manner. And this simplification may extend over the treatment of almost every disease which is spoken of in the books; so that from thirty-five to forty remedies seem amply sufficient to satisfy all the demands of a truly rational, homœopathic treatment. It is not my intention to discourage the student of homœopathy from acquiring a perfect knowledge of the Materia Medica of our School; far from it. It is a great shame that the primary sources of our art, the great and immortal works of the founder of homœopathy, and more particularly his Materia Medica Pura and his Chronic Diseases, together with the provings belonging thereto, should not be studied more zealously than they are. It is a laborious and fatiguing study, and a good deal of ingenuity and pathological science are required, to appropriate the immense number of symptoms which are detailed in those works, to one's reason and experience in such a manner that they shall become trustworthy, useful, and necessary guides in the treatment of disease. We ought not to forget that these noble works are by far the best part of our art; that our most brilliant cures are achieved with the drugs which were originally proved by Hahnemann and his first disciples; that his own provings are perfectly reliable, and that it is a most useful exercise for the mind of the student to compare the drug-symptoms as arranged by Hahnemann, with the phenomena of disease as described in the works of such men as Hufeland, Schoenlein, Watson, Canstatt, and many others, and to establish a perfect union between these two parallel orders of facts upon the permanent and incontrovertible basis of our physiological and pathological sciences. But while the student of homœopathy is engaged in this interesting business, which is, indeed, the business of a life-time, it is desirable that the benefits of homœopathy should be rendered accessible to him, and, indeed, to all who wish to avail themselves of the great blessings of our art; and it is to accomplish this end that I have embodied the results of my own investigations and experience in the present work, which may seem novel and startling to those who are in the habit of blindly and thoughtlessly following the beaten track, but which cannot fail to commend itself to all the enlightened friends of medical science, and more particularly to the honest adherents of our School, by its intrinsic truthfulness of purpose, and earnestness of reasoning. My great aim is to benefit the sick;

to popularise the homœopathic treatment by reducing it to simpler, more accurate, more positive principles; to free the homœopathic Materia Medica of a large quantity of useless and cumbersome rubbish, and to aid, as far as lies in my power, toward the superior usefulness of medicine, both as a science and an art. I doubt not that all such efforts will be ultimately crowned with success.

It must not be supposed that I am *alone in my condemnation* of that senseless agglomeration of pretended symptoms which a few superficial, conceited, and self-styled leaders of the Homœopathic school are constantly engaged, with a sort of frenzy, in conjuring up in their deluded and intoxicated imaginations, and crowding into the homœopathic Materia Medica, to the detriment of our art, and to the great annoyance of all conscientious and devoted practitioners. Hahnemann himself was just as much opposed to this unprincipled symptom-hunting mania, as any modern reformer of homœopathy. In a note to the provings of Alumina, page 35, in the second volume of the Chronic Diseases, he expresses himself as follows: "It is only with two letters, N—g., that Doctors Hartlaub and Trinks designate a man who furnished the greater number of symptoms for their Annals. His symptoms are frequently described with a careless and ambiguous prolixity. I have endeavored to extract such of them as seemed to me to be possessed of practical value, taking it of course, for granted, that he had acted as a conscientious and discreet observer." It makes very little difference, however, whether the prover's name was written in full, or whether only his initials were given. Hartlaub and Trinks were responsible for the prover's name and honesty, and Hahnemann's criticism applies not only to Alumina and most of the other antipsorics, but to most of those provings which were not instituted either by himself or under his personal supervision and direction. No more emphatic condemnation of the practices of unprincipled provers of drugs—God save the mark!—than is contained in this short rebuke from the master, could be uttered. And coming as it does, from Hahnemann, who is justly regarded as our highest authority in all such matters, it ought to serve as a warning to those deluded and vain-glorious jokers who pride themselves in parading before the world thousands of illusory symptoms, that have not the least practical value, and leave the physician, if he means to avail himself of the drug at all, no other alternative than to use it empirically in the few cases to which it seems adapted. Of what earthly use would be the provings of Lachesis, if this poison could not be used empirically? or Fluoric acid? or Glonoine? or Millefolium? or some of our boasted antipsorics, the pathogenesis of which Hahnemann himself suspected or condemned? Who cares to use Alumina, Agaricus, Dulcamara, Magnesia sulphurica, Kali nitricum, Natrum, and a host of other antipsoric remedies, in accordance with their published symptoms? If such remedies are used at all, they are either used empirically or in accordance with the indications which old-school pathologists have furnished us.

I give this work to the public as an exposition, upon the basis of inductive reasoning, of the principles of the specific homœopathic healing art. Homœopathy is, indeed, not any thing, except in so far as the remedies which it recommends for particular diseases, are specifically related to them, and, therefore, endowed with specific curative influences over the disease. This term "SPECIFIC HOMŒOPATHY," may seem startling to those who, glancing only at the letter of our great text-book, the Organon of

Hahnemann, have failed to perceive the animus of its teachings. In the 147th paragraph, Hahneman states with unmistakeable clearness, that the remedy which is truly homœopathic to the disease, is the specific remedy in this particular case. His words are, "Of all these medicines, the one whose symptoms bear the greatest resemblance to the totality of those which characterize any particular natural disease, is the most appropriate and certain homœopathic remedy that can be employed; IT IS THE SPECIFIC REMEDY IN THIS CASE." In other words, no other remedy could, properly speaking, fulfil all the conditions of a truly curative agent in this case, and a cure could not, strictly speaking, be effected in accordance with the highest demands of the true healing art, which are to cure the patient in the most expeditious, safe, and agreeable manner.

Specific homœopathic remedies do not necessarily achieve a cure in every case. Even specifics will fail of curing when the reactive energies of the organism are entirely destroyed; but specific remedies accomplish a cure in every case where a cure is possible, and much more speedily, safely and thoroughly, than any other medicine could do. A very common remedy for cough, with titillation in the larynx, is Ipecacuanha, and I have known homœopathic physicians who used it for weeks for such a trouble, without any great benefit; but it is recommended in the books, and therefore has to be used. But Ipecacuanha is not, by any means, the specific remedy for this kind of cough; the specific medicine cures it perfectly in a few days. Or take a case of chronic diarrhœa, with mucous discharges. A very common prescription for such a condition of the bowels, and which is used by a great many physicians, is Pulsatilla; and they will give it again and again in the same case, in stronger or weaker doses, without doing the patient any good. Pulsatilla cures some kinds of diarrhœa which come on suddenly, in consequence of some particular cause, perhaps an indigestion or a cold; but even in such cases, it is seldom the specific remedy. In chronic diarrhœa it scarcely ever does any good, and physicians who merely select it in accordance with the color, smell or consistence of the alvine discharges, do not do their patients justice, and invariably fail of effecting a cure; if a cure take place, it is certainly not the medicine to which the patient is indebted for it.

The specific method of treatment leads to

legitimate doubts concerning the therapeutic virtues of many drugs which have an immense number of symptoms in our Materia Medica, and yet do not seem to be adequately useful in practice. Some of these remedies, when testing their therapeutic value by the specific method, are found to be of very little, or at any rate, of only a limited use in practice; among them we may mention such remedies as Alumina, Natrum muriaticum, Agaricus, Carbo vegetabilis, Lycopodium, Sulphuric and Nitric acid, the north and south pole of the magnet, and a number of other drugs, more particularly among the recent additions to our Materia Medica. I am fully aware that cures are pretended to have been effected with all these drugs; but I doubt the correctness of many of these observations. Even such boasted remedies as Sulphur, Antimonium, Sepia, Calcarea and many others find their sphere of action considerably narrowed down by the specific method. And this must be a great relief to all thinking homœopathic practitioners; for what homœopathic physician would have dared to conduct the cure of a chronic case without Sulphur, or of a scrofulous disease without Calcarea? As the lancet and the leech had become emphatically the antiphlogistica of the

Old School, so had Sulphur become the antipsoricum "par excellence," and Calcarea the antiscrofulous panacea of homœopathy; and I am very much afraid that both Sulphur and Calcarea, although they will not fare quite as badly as the lancet and the leech, will be found to have been in possession of truly royal privileges, which the progress in rational medicine will compel them to forego. Sulphur, Calcarea, Sepia, Acidum nitricum, Acidum sulphuricum, Lycopodium, Kali carbonicum, Kali nitricum, and a large number of other drugs, especially among the so-called antipsorics, have now been in use for many years, some of them twenty-five and thirty years, and yet, few of their symptoms, comparatively speaking, have ever been met with in practice, although these medicines have been used by thousands of homœopathic physicians in every country, and in millions of cases. What is the unavoidable inference to be drawn from such facts? Do not these facts go to show that a great many remedies contained in these immense lists of symptoms, are either imaginary or that their importance has, at any rate, been over-rated; that the true, essential, positive, or, in one word, specific sphere of action of a drug, is limited to a very small number of symptoms, and that the trifling ailments which are recorded in company with its leading and essential effects, with the most rigid dogmatism and pedantic importance, have no further value than to give pre-eminence to the really positive and essential symptoms, and to enable an observing practitioner to determine the starting-point of the drug's action in the organism, with scientific accuracy? It is impossible to impress with too much emphasis upon our provers the necessity of discriminating between the symptoms which make their appearance during the course of an experimentation. A great many of them do not belong to the drug at all. And many others, although belonging to the drug, yet do not point to any distinct disease, and should simply be looked upon as general indications of the non-homogeneity of the drug-action, and the essential principles of the normal organism. These symptoms simply indicate, that the drug is a substance which disagrees with the organism in the same sense as certain otherwise perfectly healthy articles of food do not agree with many persons, and cause all sorts of ailments, sick-headaches, cardialgia, colic, diarrhœa, nausea or vomiting, etc. It would be wrong to suppose that these same articles must, on this account, prove efficacious as remedial agents when such affections occur to the same individuals from other causes. My own experience, at least, does not warrant any such general conclusions, although I am willing to admit exceptions. Almost every drug causes such general derangements as headache, vomiting, diarrhœa, colic, and so forth; but it would be wrong to suppose that every drug will, on this account, prove curative in the above mentioned affections. It is doubtful whether the carbonate of Magnesia has ever cured a case of headache, except upon revulsive principles; the same may be said of the nitrate of Potash, of Sulphuric acid, and a number of other drugs, all of which are said to produce headache, but are never employed in such an affection. Why? Because a secret instinct seems to tell practitioners that these drugs will prove ineffectual, if used as remedies for headache. And this observation applies to every other series of symptoms, to the gastric symptoms, the various secretions, the cutaneous alterations, the symptoms of the intellectual and emotive sphere, etc. What physician ever dreams of using Alumina in a case of mental derangement, or Crocus in a case of rheumatism? And yet, a number of symptoms is recorded of either drug, and indeed of almost any other drug, which might be construed into indications for the cure of mania or rheumatism. The common sense of physicians has assigned to each drug a certain sphere of action, beyond which it is scarcely ever employed; and, although such demarcations should be strictly conformable to the demands of rigorous physiological experimentation, yet the principle which this species of routine-practice embodies, is correct, namely: that drugs have specific spheres of action, and that this specific action is revealed by positive, essentially true and unchanging symptoms. All these symptoms are more or less reproduced in every case of proving, no matter where the prover may reside, or what his age or sex may be, except of course such drugs as affect the sexual sphere; and symptoms which are not more or less experienced by every prover, should be looked upon with great suspicion; they may be the result of a peculiar idiosyncratic relation between the prover and the drug, but they should not be admitted as genuine effects of the drug, without the greatest circumspection. What has been said of the symptoms of the same drug, applies with equal force to the different drugs themselves. It seems to me a self-evident truth, that drugs occupy a different rank amongst each other as curative agents. What philosophical physician would rank Lycopodium on a par with Arsenic or Belladonna? The action of such drugs as Aconite, Belladonna, Nux vomica, Phosphorus, and many others, is of a more intense quality than the action of Sepia, Lycopodium, Silex, Magnesia, and I infer from this incontestable fact, that the effects of the former series of drugs are more marked, more characteristic, and therefore more reliable as curative indications. Suppose Arsenic and Natrum muriaticum should seem equally strongly indicated in a certain case, I should undoubtedly give the preference to Arsenic, and I should base my preference upon the inherent superiority of Arsenic over Natrum as a remedial agent. The substances which are used as drugs, have various degrees of inherent remedial power, proportionate to their more or less absolute character as remedial agents. Aconite possesses a higher degree of inherent medicinal power than Natrum muriaticum, for this reason, that the former is a drug in an absolute sense, whereas, the latter fulfils mixed uses, among which its properties as a culinary agent are much more remarkable than its remedial virtues. Indeed, it is highly questionable whether the sphere of its remedial action is at all as extensive as it is supposed to be, and whether the boasted richness of its symptoms is not on a par with the pathogenesis of fluoric acid, bromine, lachesis and the like, all grandiloquent sounds and moonshine. It is to be hoped that the time is fast approaching when the minds of homœopathic practitioners will be emancipated from the degrading thraldom of childish symptom-hunters; when homœopathy will cease to be a science of inglorious illusions, and when the living, unerring truths of experience and reason will be substituted in their stead.

THE

Twelve Golden Rules,

WHICH SHOULD BE FOLLOWED

By all who wish to Preserve their Health,

AND MORE PARTICULARLY

BY THOSE WHO FAVOR THE

Homœopathic Treatment of Disease.

THE

TWELVE GOLDEN RULES,

WHICH SHOULD BE OBSERVED BY EVERY BODY,

But more particularly by persons who are under Homœopathic Treatment, or who habitually resort to it in sickness, or generally favor the Homœopathic doctrines and mode of practice.

In all acute diseases, the diet and general treatment of the patient is, of course, strictly regulated by the attending physician or nurse, agreeably to the exigencies of the case; the following rules are designed only for persons in health, or for chronic patients whose general health seems satisfactory, or for all those who are not obliged, by particular circumstances, to deviate from them.

Rule 1.

Rise early, and make it a point to retire at ten o'clock; seven hours' sleep should suffice; although less may do in some cases, and, in others, more may be required.

Rule 2.

Wash your whole body from head to foot, with cold water, every morning, winter and summer, immediately after leaving the bed; and rub yourself well with a flesh-brush or coarse towel, immediately after washing.

Rule 3.

Never sleep in a warm room, or in a room that has not been properly ventilated in the day-time.

Rule 4.

Never sit or sleep in a draught of air; this rule is almost universally violated, but a draught of air is generally hurtful, more in one case than in another, and more especially when persons are over-heated, or covered with perspiration.

Rule 5.

Dress according to the season; but be careful not to leave off your winter clothes before the warm weather has fairly set in. This rule should be particularly observed by persons who are subject to sore throat, bronchitis, chronic cough, and such like weaknesses.

Rule 6.

Avoid all kinds of heavy and indigestible food, such as rich pastry, fat, heavy farinaceous diet, warm bread, spices, mustard, pepper, etc.

Rule 7.

Avoid all stimulating drinks, brandy, beer, wine, and content yourself with cold water, milk, light and unspiced chocolate, weak black tea, and syrups made of currants, raspberries, strawberries, or other kinds of wholesome and unmedicinal fruit. Never use tobacco in any shape, except for medicinal purposes.

Rule 8.

Never keep on wet or damp clothes, stockings, etc., and never sleep on damp sheets.

Rule 9.

Do not expose yourself to keen, sharp winds, and avoid the raw and damp evening air.

Rule 10.

Live as nearly as possible in the same temperature; keep your room moderately warm, and make it a point never to sit near the fire.

Rule 11.

Eat your meals at regular hours; eat slowly; chew every mouthful well, and do not swallow it until it is properly mixed up with saliva. If possible, take about an hour for each meal, and never eat so much as to leave the table with a sense of repletion and oppression; do not forget to clean your teeth with a soft tooth-brush after eating, and never indulge in the abominable habit of picking them.

Rule 12.

Avoid every kind of food or drink which naturally disagrees with you; take a little exercise in the open air every day, but not in any kind of weather; select particularly fine, bracing or balmy weather for a walk or ride; exposure to rainy, windy, raw or damp weather never does any body any good.

These twelve rules are golden rules, the observance of which can never be impressed with too much care upon the attention of those who are anxious to preserve their health, and to remain free from the many unpleasant feelings which are apt to trouble those who neglect the proper dietetic and hygienic precautions.

The followers of Hahnemann should all be distinguished by habits of cleanliness, neatness and regularity, and by moderation in the use of food and drink; every genuine homœopathist will consider it his duty to cultivate a refined taste in manners, language, feelings and habits of life, and he will use all his influence to discourage the sad and devastating practices of chewing, smoking and drinking, to which so many millions are addicted to the detriment of their health and the ruin of their fortunes and inward peace.

PART I.

HOMŒOPATHY PROPER,

OR

THE HOMŒOPATHY OF SYMPTOMS.

PART I.

Hahnemann's Organon is undoubtedly the great text-book of the Homœopathic School. It would be just as futile to undertake to practise homœopathy without having previously acquired a thorough and logical knowledge of the doctrines embodied in the Organon, as it would be to attempt to become a perfect mathematician without a knowledge of the theorem of Pythagoras, or an astronomer without being acquainted with the laws of Keppler. Those who wish to acquire an accurate and comprehensive knowledge of the doctrines of the Homœopathic School as taught by Hahnemann, have to seek this knowledge in the richly freighted pages of the Organon. To be sure, what has so often happened in religion and law, may likewise happen, and unfortunately has happened in homœopathy: the apparent meaning of the literal text has been mistaken for the real, living doctrine, and dead formulas, emanating from human conceit and the deceitful illusions of the sensual understanding may triumph for a time over the eternal and boundlessly expansive reason. But then it is not the

Organon that should be held responsible for such adulterations of its deep and momentous truths. It is upon the unreasoning pride and cunning of those who profess to tread in the footsteps of Hahnemann, that all such perversions should be charged; let us hasten to emancipate the free spirit from the dogmatic pedantry which now holds it captive; and to elevate our doctrine from a mere human system, to which its magnificent proportions had been reduced by the blind and stubborn obscurantism of a few self-constituted leaders, to the rank which it undoubtedly occupied in Hahnemann's own mind, and which it possesses in the living mechanism of nature, to the rank of an absolute, unerring, eternally-progressive science.

In order to do full justice to the task which I have proposed to fulfil, I will give a succinct statement of the rules and doctrines which make up the sum and substance of the Organon. I shall not deem it necessary, however, to transfer to these pages Hahnemann's searching criticism of the old fashioned modes of treatment, nor the mass of testimony which he has extracted from allœopathic writers in confirmation of the truth of his own doctrine. Those who are anxious to become acquainted with these highly interesting and valuable facts, will find them recorded in the first part of the Organon. My duty here consists in explaining the synthetical portion of the work in a logical form, and in strict obedience to the meaning which Hahnemann seems to have embodied in his text.

HAHNEMANN'S DEFINITION OF DISEASE.

Hahnemann is professedly a vitalist. In the 9th paragraph of the Organon, he expresses himself as follows: "In the healthy condition of man, the immaterial vital principle which animates the material body, exercises an absolute sway and maintains all its parts in the most admirable order and harmony, both of sensation and action, so that our indwelling rational spirit may freely employ these living, healthy organs for the superior purposes of our existence.

"The material organism deprived of its vital principle, is incapable of sensation, action, or self-preservation; it is the immaterial vital principle only, animating the former in its healthy and morbid condition, that imparts to it all sensation, and enables it to perform its functions."

Disease arises from, or rather consists in, a disturbance of the harmonious action of the vital principle caused "by the dynamic influence of a morbific agent which is inimical to life." Hahnemann expresses this idea more fully in Sect. II. of the Organon in the following language: "In disease, the spontaneous and immaterial vital principle pervading the physical organism, is primarily deranged by the dynamic influence of a morbific agent which is inimical to life, only the vital principle thus disturbed, can impart to the organism its abnormal sensations, and incline it to the irregular actions which we call disease; for as an invisible principle which is only cognizable through its operations in the organism, its morbid disturbances can be perceived solely by means of the morbid sensations and actions of the organism which are perceptible to the senses of the physician and bystanders; in other words, by the *morbid symptoms*, and can be indicated in no other manner."

These perceptible symptoms, and the actual disturbance of the vital action are so much alike, that they may be looked upon as an unitary, inseparable, morbid condition. This is manifestly meant by the following statement in Sect. XV. of the Organon: "the sufferings of the immaterial vital principle which animates the interior of our bodies, and the mass of symptoms produced by it in the organism, which are externally manifested, and represent the actual malady, constitute a whole, they are one and the same. The organism is, indeed, the material instrument of life; but without that animation which is derived from the instinctive sensibility and control of the vital principle, its existence is as inconceivable as that of a vital principle, without an organism; consequently, both constitute an unit, although, in order to facilitate our comprehension, our minds may separate this unit into two distinct ideas."

Nevertheless, although Hahnemann does not object to this separation of the perceptible symptoms and the morbid state which they represent; and, although he looks upon disease as a disturbance of the vital harmony of the organism by the influence of some foreign heterogeneous agent: yet it must not be supposed, on that account, that disease is a peculiar and distinct something in the human organism. "Disease," says Hahnemann in Sect. XIII. of the Organon, "considered as it is by the Allœopathic School as something distinct and separate from the living organism and from the vital principle which animates it, as something hidden internally and as something material, how subtle soever its nature may be supposed, is a nonentity, which for ages has given to medicine all those pernicious deviations that constitute it a mischievous art."

These various statements seem to imply a contradiction; but upon a closer examination it will be found that Hahnemann reasons consistently. As there is no life without a vital principle and without an organism which is its necessary material embodiment or form, so there is no disease without a morbific principle and the phenomena which constitute its form in the living organism. The morbific principle is of the same order or quality as the vital principle itself, and is similarly related to the organism. Allœopathic physicians have been in the habit of looking upon disease as a mass of impurities scattered through the living organism; as a vast dung-hill, if you please, that had to be swept out of the organism by physical force as it were, driven out by the skin by means of sudorifics, expelled from the bowels by purgatives, ejected from the stomach by emetics. All such gross notions are very properly rebuked by

Hahnemann, and yet, a truth is embodied in the doctrine that disease is the result of an invasion of the living organism by some hostile morbific agent. In the third part of this work, this view of disease will be elucidated more fully, and substantiated by more comprehensive reasonings.

THE TOTALITY OF THE SYMPTOMS CONSTITUTES THE WHOLE OF THE DISEASE.

In a curative point of view the totality of the symptoms constitutes the disease. In Sections VI. and XVIII. of the Organon, this doctrine is laid down in the following emphatic and unmistakeable language: "The unprejudiced observer, however great may be his powers of penetration, aware of the futility of all elaborate speculations that are not confirmed by experience, perceives in each individual affection nothing but changes of the state of the body or mind (*traces of disease, phenomena, symptoms,*) that are discoverable by the senses alone, that is to say, deviations from the former sound state of health, which are felt by the patient himself, remarked by the individuals around him, and observed by the physician. The totality of these available signs represents, in its full extent, the disease itself; that is, they constitute the true and only form of it which the mind is capable of conceiving."

"From this incontrovertible truth, that, beyond the

totality of the symptoms, there is nothing discoverable in diseases by which they could make known the nature of the medicines they stand in need of, we ought naturally to conclude that there can be no other indication whatever than the totality of the symptoms in each individual case to guide us in the choice of a remedy."

Having determined in this manner in what disease consists, and how it manifests itself to the senses in a curative point of view, we have then to decide upon the best course to remove the disease; and here the question first presents itself: by what signs are we made sure beyond a doubt, that the disease is extinguished or, as Hahnemann terms it, annihilated? The answer to this question is given by Hahnemann himself in various parts of his Organon. In Sect. VII. he expresses himself as follows: "The totality of the symptoms, *this image of the immediate essence of the malady reflected externally,* is the sole or principal sign by which the disease indicates the medicines it stands in need of. The totality of the symptoms is the principal and sole object that a physician ought to have in view in every case of disease; the power of his art is to be directed against that alone in order to cure and transform it into health."

In the following paragraph, Sect. VIII., he uses this language: "It is not possible to conceive or prove by any experience, after all the symptoms of a disease, together with all its perceptible changes are removed, that there remains, or possibly can remain, any other state than a state of health, or that the morbid alterations which had taken place in the interior of the organism, have not been annihilated."

In Sect. XII. we read the following statement: "It is solely the morbidly affected vital principle which brings forth diseases, so that the expression of disease, perceptible to the senses, announces at the same time all the internal changes, that is, all the morbid disturbances of the vital principle; in short, it displays the entire disease. Consequently, after a cure is effected, the cessation of all morbid manifestations, and of all the sensible changes which are inconsistent with the healthy performance of the functions, necessarily presupposes, with an equal degree of certainty, a restoration of the vital principle to its state of integrity, and the recovered health of the whole organism."

Another clear and emphatic statement of the object of treatment is contained in Sect. XVII. of the Organon. It is expressed in the following words: "As the cure which is effected by the annihilation of all the symptoms of a disease removes at the same time the internal change upon which the disease is founded, that is to say, destroys it in its totality; it is accordingly clear, that the physician has nothing more to do than to destroy the totality of the symptoms in order to effect a simultaneous removal of the internal change, that is, to *annihilate the disease itself.*"

Nevertheless, although Hahnemann seems to express himself as though this removal of the symptoms were a mere mechanical or outside business, it is evident, from the fifth paragraph of his Organon, that this removal implies something more than a mere sensual knowledge of the morbid phenomena, and that it cannot be effected, unless we previously possess a knowledge of the *fundamental cause* of the disease. "When a cure," says Hahnemann, "is to be performed, the physician must avail himself of all the particulars he can learn, both respecting the probable *origin* of the acute malady, and the most significant points in the history of the chronic disease, to aid him in the discovery of their *fundamental cause*, which is commonly due to some chronic miasm. In all researches of this nature, he has to take into consideration the apparent state of the physical constitution of the patient, (particularly when the affection is chronic,) the disposition, occupation, mode of life, habits, social relations, age, sexual functions, etc. etc." The broad and unmistakeable declaration contained in these few lines, saves homœopathy from the stigma of being a mere science of symptoms, and the homœopathic healing art from the reproach of consisting in the mechanical drudgery of taking a record of these symptoms agreeably to a certain order, and applying to them a similarly acting remedy. It is evident that Hahnemann looks upon the perceptible phenomena of the disease as means of arriving at a knowledge of their generating cause which is, so to speak, an intellectual, unsensual fact, exclusively determinable by the pure reason, anterior to all sensual observation, and elevated into the more or less speculative region of the causative principles of nature.

METHOD OF CURE.

Having defined disease from a therapeutic point of view, and stated the object of all treatment, it behooves us to inquire into the most appropriate mode of effecting it. In the first place we see it stated in Sect. XVI. of the Organon, that the restoration of the diseased organism to health can only be effected by means of the dynamic or spiritual influence of medicines that act upon the vital energies, and whose action is communicated to every part of the organism by the universally distributed sentient nerves. And having settled the point, that cures are effected by means of drugs, we are then prepared to inquire into the most appropriate mode of using them.

According to Hahnemann, there are only three possible methods of employing medicines in diseases, the *alloeopathic or heteropathic;* the *antipathic or exanthiopathic;* and lastly the *homoeopathic.* The *alloeopathic method* has been in general use until the discovery of homoeopathy; it consists in attacking sound parts for the purpose of drawing off the malady from another quarter. Physicking the bowels to cure a sick headache, or applying an issue or a seton to remove an irritation of the thoracic viscera, are instances of allœopathic treatment.

Nature herself is incapable of curing an existing disease by one that is dissimilar; so are the most energetic medicines, when administered in accordance with the allœopathic mode of treatment, unable to remove the disease. Three different circumstances may occur when two dissimilar diseases meet in the organism.

1st. *A disease, existing in the human body, will prevent the accession of a new and dissimilar one, if the former be of an equal or superior intensity to the latter.* Thus, if a patient has the small-pox, and, while this disease is running its course, he should be attacked with scarlatina, this eruption will not show itself upon the skin until the other disease has reached its termination. According to Larry, the oriental plague never breaks out in places where scurvy prevails, nor does it ever infect those who labor under herpetic diseases. According to Jenner, the rickets prevent vaccination from taking effect, and Hildebrand informs us that persons afflicted with phthisis, are never attacked with epidemic fevers, except when the latter are extremely violent.

2d. *Or a new and more intense disease suspends a prior and dissimilar one, already existing in the body, only so long as the former continues, but it never cures it.*

If a child should be vaccinated, and should become affected with the measles three or four days after the vaccination had taken place, the vaccine pustule will not develop itself upon the skin until the eruption has reached its termination, after which the pustule will gradually make its appearance upon the arm and run its regular course of successive stages. Rainey, in the third volume of his Medical Commentaries, p. 480, relates that, in epidemic small-pox, the measles broke out among several patients four or five days after inoculation, and retarded, until their entire disappearance, the eruption of the small-pox which subsequently proceeded in a regular manner. We are informed by Tulpius, in the first book of his observations, that two children, having contracted tinea, ceased to experience any further attacks of epilepsy to which they had till then been subject; but as soon as the tinea was removed, they were again attacked as before. Other examples of this kind of suppression of a weaker by a more powerful dissimilar disease, may be found in Sect. XXXVIII. of the Organon.

3d. *Or the new disease, after having acted for a considerable time on the system, joins itself finally to the old one, which is dissimilar, whence results a complication of two different maladies, either of which is incapable of annihilating or curing the other.*

In an epidemic, where the small-pox and the measles prevailed simultaneously, one of these maladies was suspended by the other in about three hundred cases; only in one instance P. Russell met with these two dissimilar maladies in the same patient. Rainey saw the small-pox and the measles together in two little girls; and Zencke saw the cow-pox pursue its course in a regular manner conjointly with measles and purpura. For further illustrations I refer the reader to Hahnemann's Organon, Sect. XL.

Dissimilar drug-diseases in the same organism, are much more troublesome and dangerous than natural diseases. A very frequent instance of such a combination of a drug-disease with a natural malady, presents itself after the continued use of large doses of mercury in syphilis. This combination of mercurial and syphilitic symptoms constitutes a most frightful and unmanageable disease which, if not absolutely incurable, yields only to the most careful and persevering treatment.

The *antipathic or enantiopathic method* is merely palliative. This method does very well in trifling cases where, by hushing the disease for a time, we give the organism a chance to recover its reactive energies. But it is utterly inadmissible in chronic or intensely acute cases of disease. Chronic diarrhœa cannot be successfully treated with opium, nor can inveterate constipation be removed by the continued use of purgatives. Habitual weakness can no more be cured by stimulants than plethora can be moderated by repeated venesections. All such instances of palliative treatment generally aggravate the original complaint, and frequently shatter the patient's constitution.

The injurious effects of the antipathic method are accounted for upon the principle that every medicine first produces a primary effect upon the organism, which is soon followed by an opposite secondary effect, or *reaction.* This doctrine is embodied in Sect. LXIII. of the Organon: "Every agent," says Hahnemann, "that acts upon the human economy, every medicine produces some more or less notable change in the existing state of the vital powers, or creates a certain modification in the health of man for a shorter or longer period. This change is called the *primitive effect.* But our vital powers tend to oppose their energy to this influence or impression. The perceptible effect of this opposition bears the name of *secondary effect* or *reaction,*"

The organon is replete with illustrations of this double action. A hand that had been bathed in hot water, is at first much hotter than the other that had not been immersed (primitive effect); but shortly after the hand is withdrawn, it becomes cold, and, in the end, much colder than on the opposite side (secondary effect). Or an arm that had been immersed in freezing water, is at first paler and colder than the other (primitive effect); but after it is withdrawn from the water and dried, it becomes warmer than the other and sometimes even burning hot (secondary effect). Strong coffee first stimulates the faculties (primitive effect), but leaves behind it a sense of drowsiness (secondary effect). Constipation caused by opium, (primitive effect), is followed by diarrhœa (secondary effect); and evacuations produced by purgatives (primitive effect) are succeeded by costiveness which frequently lasts for several days (secondary effect). These and similar facts confirm the injurious tendency of the antipathic method. The primitive effect of the antipathic drug soon becomes extinct, and the opposite or secondary effect, or in other words the original morbid condition returns with more inveteracy than ever.

It may here be remarked incidentally that, besides the primary and secondary effects, Hahnemann distinguishes moreover *alternate effects* of medicines. These effects are contrary, or, in certain respects, accessory, to other symptoms which afterwards appear in succession. In this case they may be regarded as consecutive effects, or as marking the transition from one to the other of the different paroxysms of the primitive action.

The only remaining method is the *homœopathic* method of healing, "which employs against the totality of the symptoms of a natural disease, a medicine that is capable of exciting in healthy persons symptoms that closely resemble those of the disease itself; it is the only one that is really salutary, and which always annihilates disease, or the purely dynamic aberrations of the vital powers, in an easy, prompt and perfect manner. In this respect, nature herself furnishes the example when, by adding to an existing disease a new one that resembles it, she cures it promptly and effectually

In Sect. XLVI. of the Organon, Hahnemann furnishes a large number of illustrations of the cure of chronic diseases by the accession of another similar but more intense disease.

Small-pox has cured a multitude of diseases that were characterized by symptoms similar to its own.

Violent ophthalmia has been cured in a perfect and permanent manner by inoculation, as stated by Leroy in his Medical Treatise for the use of mothers, p. 384.

A case of blindness of two years' standing brought on by the metastasis of tinea, was, according to Klein, perfectly cured by the small-pox. See his Interpres Clinicus, p. 293.

Dysentery is one of the bad symptoms which frequently occurs in small-pox; for this reason it cures the former disease homœopathically, as in a case recorded by F. Wendt (see his Hospital report, Erlangen, 1783.)

Vaccination, whose special symptom is a swelling of the arm, cured, after its eruption, the tumefaction of an arm that was half paralyzed. (See Stevenson, in Duncan, Annals of Medicine.)

During a case of measles, a chronic, measle-shaped tetter disappeared in a prompt, durable and perfect manner, as observed by Kortum in Hufeland's Journal, Vol. XX., No. 2, page 50. A miliary eruption that covered the neck, face and arms, during a period of six years, attended with unsupportable heat, and which returned at every change of weather, was reduced to a simple swelling of the skin on the appearance of the measles; after the cessation of the tetter, the miliary eruption was cured and never reappeared. (See Rau in Hufeland's Journal XX., p. 50.)

After such evidence and examples, argues the discoverer of homœopathy, it is impossible for any reasonable physician to persevere in the ordinary allœopathic treatment, or to continue to apply remedies which attack the body in the parts that are least diseased, by exciting evacuations, counter-irritations, derivations, etc. "The facts which have been quoted," exclaims Hahnemann in Sect. LI. of his Organon, "will more than suffice to reveal to the understanding of men the great law that *cures can only be effected with medicines that are capable of exciting symptoms analogous to those of the disease itself.* And behold the advantage which man has here over rude nature whose arts are not guided by reflection! How are the homœopathic morbid powers multiplied in the various medicines which are spread over creation, all of which are at his disposal, and may be used for the relief of his suffering fellow-mortals! With these he can create morbid symptoms as varied as the countless natural diseases which they are to cure. With such precious resources at his command, there can be no necessity for those violent attacks upon the organism for the purpose of extirpating an old and obstinate disease; and the transition from the state of suffering to that of durable health is effected in a gentle, imperceptible, and often speedy manner."

The great law of cure, upon which the whole structure of homœopathy rests, is, therefore, expressed by Hahnemann in the formula: "*Similia similibus curantur*, or *like cures like*." The whole Organon is more or less devoted to an explanation of this law, and of the most appropriate method of applying it to the treatment of disease.

In Sect. XXV. of the Organon, the above generalization is defined in these terms: "Plain experience proves to us that the particular medicine whose action upon persons in health produces the greatest number of symptoms resembling those of the disease which it is intended to cure, possesses also, in reality, the power of suppressing, in a radical, prompt and permanent manner, the totality of these morbid symptoms, that is to say, the whole of the existing disease." No two medicines can be exactly similar to the same disease. Every disease can have but one medicine that is perfectly similar to it. This, at any rate, is to be inferred from Sect. CXVIII., where we are told that "each medicine produces particular effects in the human body, and no other medicinal substance can create any that are precisely similar." In the following paragraph it is likewise stated "in the same manner that each species of plant differs from all others in its external form and peculiar mode of vegetative life, its smell and taste; in the same manner that each mineral and each salt differ from others in regard to external character as well as internal chemical properties, in the same manner do all these substances likewise differ from each other in regard to their morbific effects, and, consequently, their curative powers. Each substance exercises upon the health of man a certain and particular influence which does not allow itself to be confounded with any other."

These doctrines show most clearly and emphatically that a mere vague similarity is not sufficient to render a certain remedy homœopathic to a particular disease; it must be specifically similar to the disease, in such a way that no other medicine could be similar to it in a like manner; it is only a medicine holding such perfectly specific curative relations to the disease, that properly constitutes a homœopathic remedial agent in a given case.

EXPLANATION OF THE HOMŒOPATHIC LAW.

Hahnemann is not very anxious to furnish a rational explanation of his fundamental law. To him it is an established fact, suggested and corroborated by experience. Nevertheless, he seems to feel the necessity of offering some sort of an explanation, and in Sect. XXIX. of the Organon he indulges in the following mode of reasoning to prove the validity of his therapeutic formula.

"*Every disease (which does not belong exclusively to surgery) being a purely dynamic and peculiar change of the vital powers in regard to the manner in which they accomplish sensation and action, a change that expresses itself by symptoms which are perceptible to the senses, it therefore follows, that the homœopathic medicinal agent, selected by a skilful physician, will convert it into another medicinal disease which is analogous, but rather more intense. By this means the natural morbific power which had existed previously, and which was nothing more than a dynamic power without substance, terminates, while the medicinal disease which usurps its place, being of such a nature as to be easily subdued by the vital powers, is likewise extinguished in its turn, leaving in its primitive state of integrity and health the essence or substance which animates and preserves the body.*"

This hypothesis rests upon the simple fact that the morbific power which is inherent in drugs, is greater than the disturbing power possessed by the common causes of disease. The drug possesses an absolute, positive, unchanging power of disturbing the animal economy in a determinate and unerring manner. Every genuine drug, ipecacuanha, aconite, belladonna, arsenic, etc. produces its inherent morbid effects in the animal economy, at any period of the day, and in any individual; whereas the natural morbific causes act with uncertainty and indefiniteness. In thousands of cases they have no effect at all on the organism that is exposed to them; in thousands of other cases they indeed cause a disturbance of the vital functions, but, except in the case of definite miasmatic diseases, the effects are various, even though the exposure should be the same. In one case it is typhus, in another pneumonia, and in a third dysentery; the effects vary agreeably to the state in which the constitution of the patient happens to be; but, in any event, Hahnemann considers it fully proved "that the state of health is far more susceptible of derangement from the effects of drugs than from the influence of morbific principles and contagious miasms; or what amounts to the same thing, *the ordinary morbific principles have only a conditional and often very subordinate influence, while the drugs exercise one that is absolute, direct, and greatly superior to that of the former.*" Their curative influence depends upon this fact; the drug-disease, being specifically similar and therefore specifically superior to the natural disease, absorbs, as it were, the natural disease, and reduces it from a purely spiritual to a semi-material form which the disembarrassed vital principle finds it easy to overcome and expel from the organism. This absorption, it seems to me, takes place by means of an attractive influence which the drug-disease exercises over the natural malady. Others may explain this neutralising process differently; to my mind the doctrine of attraction suggests itself as the most plausible and most correct hypothesis regarding the modus operandi of our curative agents.

NECESSITY OF PROVING DRUGS UPON THE HUMAN BODY.

It is evident that, in order to know what medicine is homœopathic to a particular disease, we have, in the first place, to ascertain what are its pure effects upon the healthy organism. In the present state of the physical sciences we have but one way of attaining this knowledge. "By a mere effort of the mind," says Hahnemann, in Sect. XX. of his Organon, "we could never discover this innate and hidden faculty of medicines, this spiritual virtue by which they are enabled to modify the state of the human body and even cure disease. It is by experience only, *by deliberate and systematic provings* of the drugs upon healthy persons that we can ultimately succeed in obtaining a knowledge of their inherent effects upon the human organism, and, consequently, that we can learn with positive certainty, what diseases such drugs are capable of curing." After having thus tried a number of simple medicines upon the healthy body, faithfully and carefully noting all the symptoms they are capable of producing as artificial morbific agents, then only shall we possess a true Materia medica, that is to say a catalogue of the pure and certain effects of drugs. Among these are the morbid elements resembling those of the natural diseases which are to be cured by them; in a word, they comprehend artificial morbid states which supply, for the similar morbid states induced by the natural causes of disease, the only true, homœopathic, id est: SPECIFIC instruments of certain and permanent cure.

This is Hahnemann's own language as embodied in Sect. CXLIII. of his Organon, and this extract is an unanswerable refutation of the foolish doctrine of a few wiseacres in the homœopathic ranks, who constantly sneer at the idea of specific homœopathy, as though Hahnemann himself had ever dreamed of its being at all possible that a remedy should be homœopathic to a disease without being at the same time the specific remedy in this particular case. If, as Hahnemann asserts in Sect. CXVIII. of his Organon, "each medicine produces particular effects in the human body, and if no other medicinal substance can create any that are precisely similar," does it not necessarily follow from this fact that, in its relations to disease, only one drug from among all the rest, can be the true remedial agent? A man is sick, and he requires to be treated. This morbid condition can only be successfully met by one remedy; or, if the disease be composed of a series of successive states, each qualitatively distinct from the other, as in the higher forms of typhus, by a series of remedies specifically corresponding to these respective states. But the doctrine of specific homœopathy is here, as in many other parts of the Organon, vindicated by Hahnemann himself, as constituting the very soul and axiom of all his teachings, and in direct opposition to those who would fain substitute in the place of this saving and sublime truth, the ridiculous sophism that typhus may be cured by pepper as well as by the deadly nightshade, or that inflammatory rheumatism will yield to kitchen salt as well as to wolf's-bane, or to the wind flower. Out upon such disgraceful and illogical balderdash!

The manner in which the proving of medicines should be conducted, is indicated with more or less completeness in the Organon, from Sect. CXXI. to Sect. CXLII. In the latter period of his life, Hahnemann recommended that these provings should be instituted with the 30th attenuations of the medicines; but the drugs which compose his grand and magnificent work, the Materia Medica Pura, were proved with massive doses of the original drug. And see the difference between the character of the symptoms recorded in this imperishable monument of the great founder of homœopathy, and those recorded in the volumes entitled Chronic Diseases. Whereas every symptom contained in the Materia Medica Pura, bears the impress of its genuine therapeutic character, the symptoms of the so-called anti-psorics can only be accepted with great doubts and reservations, and were even suspected and partially rejected by Hahnemann himself; not to mention the symptoms of latter provers, who, while drinking all the while their toddies and their coffee, exclusively employ the higher attenuations in their pretended experimentations, and whose endless symptom-lists are not only useless in a therapeutic point of view, but ridiculous and fantastic encumbrances of our Materia Medica.

HAHNEMANN'S MODE OF SELECTING A REMEDY.

The drug-symptoms with which the homœopathic physician is to cure the ailments of his patients, being known, the question then occurs, how is he to proceed in order to arrive at a knowledge of the remedy with which a cure in a particular case is to be effected?

To attain this end, the first duty of the physician is, to take a record of all the perceptible symptoms of the patient's case. In his Organon, Sect. LXXXIII. to Sect. CIV., Hahnemann gives full instructions concerning the best mode of proceeding in this first step towards a cure. They are so minute that they almost seem pedantical. The list of the questions which the physician is directed to put to the patient, extends over several pages. It would seem, from this endless interrogatory, that Hahnemann looks upon the patient as a criminal who is anxious to conceal the crime of which he is accused, and who is cross-questioned by the examining magistrate in every possible manner that cunning and ingenuity can devise for the purpose of laying bare the guilt of the accused. I should think that any patient who is able to go through such a searching interrogatory as Hahnemann wishes to inflict upon him, must have more nerve and composure than are generally possessed by a sick man. To give the reader an idea of the strictness and minuteness with which the examination of the patient is to be conducted, I will transcribe a single paragraph from among the whole number that Hahnemann has devoted to this subject; it is Sect. LXXXIX. of the Organon. "How often have the bowels been evacuated, and what was the nature of the discharges? Did the whitish discharges consist of mucus or fæces? Were they painful or otherwise? What was the precise nature of these pains, and in what part were they felt? What did the patient throw up? Is the bad taste in the mouth putrid, bitter, or acid, or what kind of taste is it? Does he experience this taste before, during, or after eating or drinking? At what part of the day does he feel it in particular? What kind of taste was connected with the eructation? Is the urine turbid at first, or does it only become so after standing a while? Of what color was it at the time of emission? What was the color of the sediment? Is there any peculiarity in the state of the patient when he sleeps? Does he sigh, moan, speak or cry out? Does he start in his sleep? Does he move during an inspiration or expiration? Does he lie on his back only, or on which side does he lay himself? Does he cover himself up close, or does he throw off the bed-covering? Does he wake easily, or does he sleep too soundly? How does he feel on waking? How often does this or that symptom occur, and on what occasion? Is it when the patient is sitting up, lying down, standing up, or when he is moving about? Does it come on merely when he has been fasting, or at least early in the morning, or simply in the evening, or only after meals, or if at other times, when? When did the shivering come on? Was it merely a sensation of cold, or was he actually cold at the time? In what part of the body did the patient feel cold? Was his skin warm when he complained of being cold? Did he experience a sensation of cold without shivering? Did he feel heat without the face being flushed? What parts of his body were warm to the touch? Did the patient complain of heat without his skin being warm? How long did the sensation of cold, or that of heat, continue? When did the thirst come on? During the cold or heat, or was it before or after? How intense was the thirst? What did the patient ask for to drink? When did the perspiration come on? Was it at the commencement or at the expiration of the heat? What space of time elapsed between the heat and the perspiration? Was it when sleeping or waking that it manifested itself? Was it strong or otherwise? Was the perspiration hot or cold? On what parts of the body did it break out? How did it smell? What did the patient complain of before or during the cold, during or after the heat, during or after the perspiration, etc." Does it not seem as though many of these questions might be dispensed with without injury to the patient? And, if we consider that this long list of questions is scarcely the fourth part of the whole interrogatory, does it not seem as though this prolix mode of questioning were tantamount to putting the patient on the rack? I confess that, with all due deference to Hahnemann's experience, I cannot bend myself to his judgment in this mode of tracing out, as he terms it, an image of the disease, and I consider every physician who deems it necessary to institute such a diffuse examination of his patient's case, deficient either in a sufficient amount of natural talent or acquired information to be a competent homœopathic practitioner.

Knowing the symptoms of the disease, the physician then applies himself to selecting a remedy from among the whole number of the drugs whose effects upon the healthy organism have been ascertained more or less completely by a variety of provers. On this subject the Organon likewise contains ample instructions which the reader will find recorded in a series of paragraphs from Sect. CL. to Sect. CCII. A vast amount of intensely logical, interesting and highly important reasoning is embodied in these paragraphs; the treatment of diseases characterised by striking symptoms, or of such as are poorly provided with symptoms, or exhibit only one or two local symptoms, is described with a most praise-worthy foresight and minuteness; and yet I feel compelled to demur to the philosophy of Hahnemann's reasoning in this business of curing, but shall defer my objections to the second part of this work which is intended as a systematic criticism on what appears to me the objectionable features in the mode which Hahnemann and some of his followers have adopted, of explaining the homœopathic doctrines.

Enough has been said of these doctrines to make it appear, that the homœopathic method of treatment avoids all revulsions or counter-irritations; that the homœopathic remedial agent acts upon the disease in a most direct manner, and overcomes it, not by the influence of brute force, but by the superior attractiveness of its inherent power, to which the disease yields implicit and voluntary obedience. This being the case, it is evidently of the utmost importance that the inherent power of the drug should be presented to the disease in a form that will enable the remedial agent to exercise its curative influence in the safest, most direct and most expeditious manner. The adaptation of the crude drug to remedial purposes is one of the characteristic features of the homœopathic healing art, and deserves a passing notice in this place.

GENERAL METHOD OF PREPARING HOMŒOPATHIC ATTENUATIONS.

Homœopathic physicians use nearly the same medicines that have been or are used in allœopathic practice. They avoid all artificial compounds, except such as are of a purely chemical nature. In other respects they prepare their tinctures and essences pretty much in the same manner as allœopathic pharmaceutists are in the habit of doing. The original tinctures are generally termed mother-tinctures in homœopathic practice. From these mother-tinctures so-termed attenuations or potencies are derived in accordance with the rules which Hahnemann lays down with the most rigorous exactitude and minuteness at the close of the first volume of his chronic diseases. These attenuations are made with alcohol. A drop of every succeeding attenuation contains the one-hundredth part of a drop of the next preceding one. Successive attenuations are obtained by mixing one drop of any given attenuation with ninety-nine drops of alcohol and agitating this mixture by means of a series of powerful strokes of the hand that holds the vial, upon some elastic cushion. Metals or minerals, and various kinds of vegetable substances which, in their original form, cannot be dissolved in alcohol or water, are first triturated in a porcelain mortar, with sugar of milk, in the proportion of one grain of the original drug to ninety-nine grains of sugar of milk, and it is only on making the fourth attenuation that alcohol can be substituted for the sugar of milk. The effect of these successive succussions and triturations, is supposed to be a progressive development and consequent increase of the inherent medicinal power of the drug. In accordance with this fact, religiously accepted as such by a majority of homœopathic physicians, the peculiar mode which Hahnemann first proposed of converting crude drugs into remedial agents and adopting them to therapeutic purposes, has been not inaptly termed "the potentization or dynamisation of drugs," and the attenuations so obtained are frequently termed "potencies or dynamisations." This being a cardinal doctrine in homœopathy, it may not be inappropriate to present some more extensive developments concerning this interesting subject, and to throw out a few logical hints regarding the philosophy and scientific character of a doctrine that has led to many bitter discussions among homœopathic physicians themselves, and has cast on their practice an immense amount of ridicule, and in very many instances, honest contempt.

ON DYNAMISATIONS, OR POTENCIES.

In a work of this kind it cannot be expected that the arguments brought forward in support or condemnation of Hahnemann's doctrine of potentisation should be reproduced in their totality; all I have to do, in order to fulfil my duty to the reader, is to state what were Hahnemann's opinions regarding this subject; for, as yet, the science of homœopathy seems to be confined to the limits and definitions which characterised it during the earlier period of its existence.

According to Hahnemann, the curative virtue of a drug is rendered more active by destroying the cohesion of its constituent particles in the manner prescribed by him, and very fully described in the first volume of his Chronic Diseases. The inherent spirit or principle of the medicinal agent is set free, as it were, by the process of succussion and trituration, and is made available for purposes of treatment by temporarily connecting it with some neutral body, such as sugar of milk, alcohol or water. It would seem as though the curative influence or force detached itself more readily from such a neutral body and acted more promptly upon the disease. This is not to be understood as though the original molecules of the drug were entirely deprived of their essential medicinal properties; as I understand this doctrine of Hahnemann, he simply means to affirm that this power is in a great measure transmitted, as it were, to the neutral vehicle, and, not being essentially or inherently united with it as it originally was with the crude drugs, it will act so much more readily upon the disease to which it is inherently, that is, qualitatively similar. With the best will I cannot see any thing so very ridiculous in this doctrine, IF PROPERLY UNDERSTOOD, and the time may yet come when it will be proven by experimental science, that Hahnemann was right in priding himself upon this part of his great work, with the modesty which it behooves a great reformer and man of genius to display in all things and under any circumstances.

It is in this sense only, it seems to me, that Hahnemann and most of his disciples believe that the medicinal power which resides in a drug, is not only developed, but actually rendered more intense, intrinsically heightened by their peculiar mode of preparing homœopathic attenuations. Hahnemann has termed this intrinsic increase or heightening of the inherent power of a drug, by means of the processes of trituration and succussion, "*potentisation* or *dynamization*," and the peculiar mode in which he has recorded his opinions in regard to the development of the curative powers of a drug, induced by those processes, has led to the belief, that the longer those processes are continued through a successive series of attenuations, the more powerful becomes the preparation. I have frequently been asked by patients who had heard or read something of potentisation, potencies, and so forth, whether the use of highly potentised drugs was not attended with danger in particular cases. There is another erroneous impression, which has been caused by the doctrine of dynamization, and which might prove a serious obstacle to the progress of homœopathy, if this science were not founded in the providence of God, and must, therefore, eventually triumph over all opposition. It is insinuated by the opponents of the homœopathic practice, that homœopathic physicians use the most concentrated poisons, and that their medicines gradually corrupt the body and establish a principle of decay and putrefaction in the very marrow of the bones. Alloeopathic physicians of high repute and character could be named, who make themselves guilty of such gross misrepresentations. At one time it was asserted, that homœopathic physicians administered nothing but sugar of milk, or water; this argument having failed in crushing the homœopathic system, its unfair opponents have shifted to the opposite tack, and represent homœopathic preparations as the most dangerous and concentrated poisons. The fault of these absurd accusations and exaggerated statements regarding the power of homœopathic medicines, rests, in a great measure with Hahnemann and some of his disciples, for they have asserted, time and again, that homœopathic preparations could be made sufficiently powerful to destroy the lives of the patients; and Hahnemann mentions a case of whooping-cough, where the child came near losing its life by the sixtieth attenuation or potency of Drosera. But Hahnemann, with all his transcendent genius, probably labored under the same illusion with which so many physicians and laymen are afflicted, namely, that the phenomena which make their appearance after the exhibition of a medicine, must necessarily result from its action upon the patient's organism. After the administration of Drosera, in the above case, a violent paroxysm did most certainly occur; but is it not more than probable that this paroxysm was a natural development of the disease, and that it had no more to do with the action of Drosera than with the sixtieth potency of any other medicine?

A truly scientific conception of the therapeutic character of a drug is perfectly consistent with the idea that the medicinal power inherent in the crude drug, is essentially increased by the mode of preparation employed by Hahnemann; in other words, that the different potencies which are developed out of the original substances, are in the same relation to each other as the terms of a geometrical progression; but if this be true, it does not, by any means justify the conclusion, that if the power of the first term be equivalent to two, that of the second term must be equivalent to four, that of the third to sixteen, and thus *ad infinitum*. The powers of the different potencies which constitute a series, cannot be expressed numerically, but, being of a purely dynamic character, are in dynamic relations to each other, to which no mathematical exponents can be affixed, and the respective value of which has to be determined by observation, and depends altogether upon the idiosyncratic peculiarities, the disposition and receptivity of the patient. In one case it may be proper to use the tincture of a medicine, whereas in another case, although of a similar nature, a preparation of a far different dynamic power may be required. The term "potency," as applied to the homœopathic preparation, has therefore a relative meaning; it simply means that the physician should use the medicine which seems to be indicated in the case, in such quantity and form as corresponds as nearly as possible to the receptivity of the patient's organism, or more particularly his nerves. For, it is, after all, through the nervous system that all therapeutic action upon the disease has to be effected. Taking this view of potency, and this is the only true and scientific definition of the term, it will be easily understood why a whole vialful of globules, moistened with the 30th attenuation of Aconite, might have no effect on a patient, whereas one or two drops of the tincture would perhaps produce a sensible change in his condition.

Our patients frequently express their astonishment at the absence of all evil consequences which they think should result from swallowing a quantity of globules moistened with the higher preparations of some particular medicine. Their faith in the efficacy of homœopathic medicines is seriously shaken in consequence of this non-occurrence of some frightful commotion. They are accustomed to see some effect produced by medicine; they expect to be affected by the medicine in some shape or other. A great many will ask on receiving medicine from the doctor: Doctor, what will this medicine do to me? How do you intend it is to affect me? It is not always easy to quiet such patients by evasive answers, or by merely telling them that the office of a remedial agent is not to produce medicinal effects, but simply to cure disease without inflicting any additional suffering. An intelligent person may perhaps be made to understand that disease being a dynamic state and the medicine being a dynamic power, the action of the latter is absolutely and directly curative, an action of relief, and by no means intended to induce an artificial drug-disease, characterised by phenomena of disturbance of the general functions of the organism. It is sometimes very difficult to get along with inquisitive patients, and it is impossible to indicate a general course of conduct in regard to them. A physician who has acquired a philosophical perception of his doctrine, and has developed it to his own understanding out of the inmost depths of reason, will never be at a loss to answer the most pointed and embarrassing questions put to him.

In the present state of the physical sciences, the

safest position which homœopathic physicians can take in regard to their peculiar mode of preparing their medicines, is, to assert what no one can deny, that the inherent medicinal power of the drug is developed and rendered more active by breaking up the cohesion of its molecules, and that the freedom and directness with which the inherent power is enabled to influence the disease, increase in proportion to the completeness and accuracy with which the breaking up of the material molecules is accomplished. Latterly, this breaking up has been carried to a very high degree, and has given origin to what is termed the high potencies. Theoretically, it would seem as though the breaking up of the constituent particles of the drug, might be continued to an unlimited extent; but is this possible practically? This possibility is beyond the reach of physical demonstration. We do not know at all, whether any thing of the substance or spirit of Arsenic is present in the 8000th potency; we can only know this by the nicest observations at the sick-bed, and it must, therefore, be admitted, that the cures which are recorded as having been effected with the high potencies, should be received with great caution.

We can prove, by the most indubitable evidence, that the power of a drug is developed by breaking up its constituent particles. We know that a whole onion, for instance, has scarcely any effect upon the senses, whereas the emanations which arise from a comminuted onion, have a most irritating effect upon the eyes and the Schneiderian membrane. It is the same with pepper, mustard, and a variety of other substances whose internal properties and powers remain hidden as long as the cohesion of the constituent particles is not destroyed. In breaking up these particles for the purpose of developing the inherent powers of the drug, it is of the utmost importance to observe certain precautions. Nothing should get lost during the process of trituration. An onion, for instance, could not be triturated without the escape of a large quantity of active power which might be of great therapeutic value. Substances containing much volatile or aromal matter, such as onion, coffee, pepper, &c., should be immersed in dilute alcohol while the breaking up of their particles is being accomplished.

The propriety of potentising such substances beyond certain limits, may justly be doubted. Are not the aromal emanations arising from their comminuted particles, the necessary vehicles of the medicinal powers with which those substances are endowed? Is this aromal principle developed by the process of potentisation, or is it not rather diminished by it, and is it not finally altogether destroyed? In respect to these points the minds of many practitioners are in a state of doubt, and until these doubts, which appear to me perfectly legitimate, can be cleared by the evidence of experimental demonstration, it might be well to use the recent tinctures and lower triturations of all such substances as are endowed with a considerable quantity of volatile aromal matter.

The thing is different with regard to those drugs

that contain little or no volatile or aromal matter, whose particles cohere very firmly. These may have to go through a successive series of triturations before their particles are thoroughly broken up and the medicinal power which they contain, is fully developed. Arsenic, for instance, in its crude state, is a powerful poison, but of very little use in the treatment of disease. By breaking up the original particles, the chemical or poisonous powers of the drug are diminished, and adapted to therapeutic purposes. In proportion as a medicinal substance is, in its crude state, endowed with powerful poisonous properties, it admits of a higher degree of potentisation for the determination of its curative powers. The same remark applies to medicinal agents which, in their crude state, are more or less inert. Such agents are, for instance, lycopodium, silex, carbo, etc.

Dr. Streintz, of Germany, has instituted microscopical observations with several triturations of lycopodium, and found that, in one case, where the trituration had been prepared by an allœopathic pharmaceutist, all the seeds were left entire ; in another case the largest number of the seeds was left unbroken ; and in a few cases only were all the seeds properly crushed. He says furthermore that, if a portion of the first trituration be mixed with water, the crystals of the sugar of milk will dissolve, and the fragments of the crushed lycopodium remain behind in a state of integrity, consisting of small portions of the perisperm, of irregular portions of seed, and a large quantity of very small drops of oil. The same ingredients are discovered in the second and third triturations, except that these particles are smaller and less numerous.

The theory of potentisation, as laid down by Hahnemann, has been a thing of gradual growth. One of the first causes which led to the potentising process, is the peculiar view which Hahnemann took of the modus operandi of remedial agents administered agreeably to the law "similia similibus curantur." According to Hahnemann the homœopathic agent sets up a dynamic action in the organism, similar to, but more powerful than, the natural disease, which is easily overcome by its antagonist. The natural disease being overcome, the action of the homœopathic agent ceases without occasioning any further artificial disturbance of the organism.

Hahnemann supposed, from theory much more than from actual observation, that there was danger of increasing the violence of the natural disease, if a similar pathological state should be superadded to it by the homœopathic agent. And being furthermore impressed with the conviction, that disease was a dynamic or spiritual state, and has therefore to be acted upon dynamically by a substance, which, by means of adequate manipulations, had been transformed as nearly as possible into a spiritual power, he could not fail in proposing the mode of preparation he adopted, as the most adequate to accomplish the spiritualising process which he considered absolutely necessary in order to raise the crude drug to the rank of a true therapeutic agent. Hahnemann reasoned, as a matter of course, that, if the homœopathic agent were given in too large a dose, the natural disease would be increased by it; and the only way in which the dose could be reduced to a proper size, was the mode which the great reformer adopted, of *attenuating* as he then termed it, the original medicine. This method of attenuating drugs, was altogether a novel proceeding, unknown before Hahnemann, and must have seized upon his mind with all the force of a magic spell. The law of cure had been known before him in isolated cases, but it had been thrown away as a child would ignorantly throw away a precious jewel; he presented the law as an universal principle, and applied it as such to the treatment of disease; but the process of attenuation was his own invention, his property as it were, and must, therefore, have filled his mind with more than ordinary interest, perhaps beyond the bounds of impartial reason. Not that Hahnemann was vain; I take it upon myself to absolve him from all accusations of vanity; but Hahnemann was a man, a fallible man, and driven onward by the bugbear of medicinal aggravations, may have seen fit to continue the attenuating process in many instances further than there was any necessity for. He may likewise have been desirous of ascertaining the degree up to which the sick organism remained susceptible to the action of a homœopathic agent, and finding that, in some instances at least, this susceptibility had scarcely any limits, he may have concluded with a generous rashness, that it was best, under all circumstances, to attenuate or potentise medicines to a very high degree before using them in practice. It behooves us to identify our minds as much as possible with the circumstances under which Hahnemann developed his doctrines; this will enable us to construct them for ourselves independently of the bend of the master's mind, to separate the wheat from the chaff, and, having proved all things, to keep that which is good. After these few critical remarks concerning the dynamization of drugs, we may safely admit,

1. That the inherent power of a drug is developed by breaking up its component particles;

2. That this breaking up can, in the case of a number of drugs, be carried to a very high degree;

3. That, in many cases, it requires a considerable number of successive developments of power as pointed out by Hahnemann, to obtain a preparation which shall adequately correspond to the susceptibilities of the patient's organism and to the quality of the disease, and effect a safe and speedy cure;

4. That the term "potency" should only be used qualitatively, as expressive of the curative adaptation of a certain remedial agent to a given cure of disease in a given organism.

GENERAL PRINCIPLES INVOLVED IN THE USE OF HOMŒOPATHIC PREPARATIONS.

Having explained the doctrine of potentisation, various questions of interest now present themselves to the mind. What potencies or attenuations should be principally used in the treatment of disease? In what form should the medicine be administered to the patient? What should be the size of the dose? How often should the dose be repeated? Is it proper to administer more than one medicine at a time? Let us review these various subjects in the order in which they are here presented.

I. What potencies or attenuations should be principally used?

Elsewhere I have alluded to this subject in the following language:—

"For convenience sake, let us divide the whole series of potencies now in use, into four classes: *lower*, *middle*, *higher* and *highest* potencies. The lower potencies range from the mother-tinctures to the sixth attenuation; the middle potencies from the sixth to the thirtieth; the higher potencies from the thirtieth to the two-hundredth; and the highest potencies to any attenuation above that grade. All these different potencies are used by their respective adherents, and proclaimed by them as the best and most useful, or rather only useful preparations. The student of medicine should not allow himself to be beguiled into a passive adherence to any one of these exclusive preferences. His duty and the interests of the sick require that he should acquaint himself with the different views now existing in the homœopathic ranks, relative to the doses which should be used in particular cases; that he should subject these views to a close and impartial investigation, adopt such of them as agree with his judgment, and reduce them to practice with caution and discrimination. The student of homœopathy should scorn to swear by the words of his master. If this blind allegiance should be required of him the master would render himself liable to the suspicion of charlatanism or unenlightened intolerance; and, on the other hand, the student who submits to this species of despotism, is entirely unfit to practice the sacred act of healing. The series of potencies is like the gamut in music. A skilful artist may indeed construct a harmony with the various vibrations of the same chord; but what a much more beautiful and perfect harmony he might construct by a proper combination of all the sounds that can be elicited from all the chords of his instrument! This is likewise true in regard to the various attenuations of a homœopathic remedial agent. Either of the four classes into which I have divided the whole series of potencies, may be sufficient, in the hands of an able practitioner, to heal the sick; but the cure will most assuredly be effected more promptly, and will be more thorough and permanent, by selecting from the whole series whatever attenuations may seem, in his independent judgment, to be suitable to the case, than by confining himself, from prejudice or habit, to one or two attenuations in preference to any other. Hahnemann, in his latter years, confined himself exclusively to the thirtieth or some higher potency. If this be true, it by no means follows that his example should be imitated. Hahnemann treated almost exclusively chronic diseases, and it is possible and even probable that in all such diseases the higher attenuations may have been sufficient.

II. In what form or mode should the medicine be administered to the patient?

Homœopathic medicines may be administered in various forms to suit the requirements of the case and the taste of the patient. They may be administered in the shape of saccharine globules impregnated with the medicine, in water, powder-form, by olfaction and likewise endermatically. The globules, may either be given dry on the tongue or dissolved in water. A very common mode of administering the medicine, is to dissolve a few globules, or one or more drops of the tincture or alcoholic attenuation in a tumblerful of water, and to give this preparation in tablespoon or teaspoonful doses. If administered by olfaction, the medicinal emanations should be sufficiently powerful to make an impression upon the Schneiderian membrane. Hahnemann, as a general rule, condemned the endermatic use of medicines. We should distinguish, however, between revulsive or counter-irritating medicines and homœopathic specifics. Counter-irritating medicines may have a tendency to suppress the cutaneous disease if applied externally; but there is every reason to believe that homœopathic specifics, may and ought, under certain circumstances, to be used endermatically for the purpose of promoting the cure. In syphilis, sycosis, and in a variety of psoric eruptions and nervous affections, the specific medicine may be safely employed externally to the great advantage of the patient. From the first, Hahnemann allowed the external use of Arnica in contusions and Thuya in sycosis. In the second edition of his anti-psoric remedies he has extended the privilege of using the remedy externally to every other medicinal substance, provided the medicine, instead of being applied directly to the diseased spot, is only applied to such portions of the skin as are free from the eruption. But why should not remedies, if applied directly to the diseased spot, act more speedily than in this round-about way? If it be at all true that, under certain circumstances, the remedies should be applied externally, then it must be true, *a fortiori*, that their curative influence is perceived the more speedily and thoroughly, the more directly they are applied to the diseased spot. The whole question, therefore, turns on this single point. Is it at all proper that remedies should be applied externally? This question might be answered by another question: Why should not remedies, under certain circumstances, act from without inwards just as well as from within outwards, or even more expeditiously and thoroughly? The inmost vital process is undoubtedly carried on from within outwards; but the vital forces are likewise affected by external influences, either pleasantly or unpleasantly. These external influences stimulate the vital forces into action; without them life would become extinct, and why should not a medicinal substance be, in certain conditions of the organism, the most appropriate stimulus for its harmonious activity, or rather for the restoration of that harmony? The precise mode of applying remedies externally in given cases, is both the business of theory and observation, and it is the office of therapeutic manuals to enlighten the student of homœopathy on this head.

III. The size of the dose.

The size of the dose has been a bone of contention among homœopathic physicians ever since the science of homœopathy was first announced by its illustrious discoverer. And it cannot be said that the discussion has been conducted with Christian forbearance. The persecutions to which homœopathic physicians had been subject on the part of their opponents, so far from teaching them charity towards each other in mere matters of opinion or unsettled experience, seem, on the contrary, to have fired them on to bitter denunciations, and to have kindled a spirit of intolerant exclusivism and unjust derision. It seems to me that the size of the dose depends principally upon the following points:

1. The intensity of the disease;
2. The degree of willingness manifested by the sick organism to receive the medicinal impression; and
3. The degree of medicinal power inherent in the remedial agent.

Starting from these conditions I generally prefer the lower attenuations

1. In all acute fevers with local inflammation or congestion;
2. In all acute intermittent fevers and all acute intermittent diseases, such as fever and ague, inflammatory neuralgia, etc.;
3. In all chronic diseases that have a tendency to terminate in disorganization of the tissues, such as syphilis, tuberculous and scrofulous swellings, etc.;
4. In nervous diseases which readily terminate in the destruction of parts, or in a permanent functional derangement of the part affected, such as the various forms of acute nervous irritation, spinal irritation,

seated or shifting congestions, spasms, convulsions, apoplexy, etc.;

5. In actual disorganizations, suppurations, ulcerations, such as blennorrhœa of the lungs, uterus, vagina; phagedenic ulcers, schirrus, hypertrophy of organs, etc.

As a general rule it is safe to employ the lower attenuations in these diseases. I say, as a general rule; for, in a number of cases of these very diseases, the middle or higher attenuations may be more conducive to a speedy and permanent cure. Physicians who practice in the same families from year to year, enjoy great advantages over the beginning practitioner as respects the dose which should be prescribed under certain circumstances. They are afforded frequent opportunities of studying the constitution of their patients, and the character of the diseases to which the members of the family are most liable, and hence they are better able to judge both the size of the dose and the medicine which is best calculated to make a curative impression upon the disease. The beginning practitioner, being deprived of these advantages of steady observation, has to steer his course in respect to doses with great caution. It being the legitimate right of every practitioner to deduce rules of practice from the clinical observations he is enabled to make, the student of homœopathy must expect to find a good deal of speculative reasoning mixed up with sound practical teaching, and to see one class of practitioners attack the statements of another class, in many cases with a good deal of bitterness of feeling. What is the student of homœopathy to do in the presence of these apparently perplexing circumstances, these contradictory statements and inferences? To the honest and intelligent student there is but one way left, and this is, to hear every side, to listen to every opinion, and then to judge for himself and pursue a perfectly independent course.

The use of the *middle* and *higher* attenuations is principally confined to

1. Acute fevers without local inflammation or congestion;

2. Purely nervous affections of a non-inflammatory character;

3. Various forms of hysteria and hypochondria without any apparent tendency to disorganization;

4. Acute affections which had been treated allœopathically by repeated depletions or violent revulsive means;

5. Chronic diseases generally, without tendency to disorganization.

These rules, though perhaps generally true, likewise admit of many exceptions. Tumors, gangrenous disorganizations, caries of bones, have disappeared under the use of the higher potencies. Syphilis has been cured with the higher as well as with the lower attenuations. Many cases of hysteria, where the higher preparations proved ineffectual, have yielded to the lower attenuations of the same drug. On the other hand, many cases of congestion or local inflammation have been much more successfully treated with the higher than with the lower potencies. And again, in many cases of acute as well as chronic disorders, the higher or lower attenuations are used indiscriminately with a like success.

The *highest* potencies are used by some practitioners in preference to any other. It cannot be denied that they have effected cures, but, on the other hand, it is admitted by all candid and philosophical practitioners that an exclusive adherence to the highest potencies is infinitely more destructive of the benefits of homœopathic treatment than an exclusive preference of the lower attenuations. My own experience leads me to doubt the efficacy of the highest potencies in chronic miasmatic diseases, in disorganizations, acute epidemic diseases, such as small-pox, scarlatina, cholera, and in acute fevers with local congestions or inflammations. Nevertheless, even in such affections, the highest potencies of some drugs may act with an astonishing promptitude and permanent success. As regards the general fact that cures have been effected with the highest potencies, it seems to me undeniable. I assert most positively that I have succeeded in effecting some brilliant cures by means of them. I have cured a case of chronic gastritis characterised by a sense of fulness at the pit of the stomach, bloating of the abdomen, loss of appetite, foul taste in the mouth, and a thickly coated tongue which the patient himself could not behold without disgust, with the two-hundredth potency of Aconite. A case of angor nocturnus, which attacked the patient every night, and was accompanied with excessive vomiting of a whitish mucus, yielded at once to two globules of the two-hundredth potency of Ipecacuanha. A case of nervous nausea which made its appearance after the cessation of an habitual buzzing in the left ear brought on by suddenly whispering some distressing news into the patient's ear, was removed on the spot by a single globule of the three-hundredth potency of Aconite. A case of habitual inveterate constipation, depending upon an irritation of the lower portion of the spinal chord, and which had been treated with cathartic medicines for more than a year past, yielded most promptly to a globule of the two-thousandth potency of Sulphur, dissolved in half a tumblerful of water. After having taken a table-spoonful of this solution, a diarrhœa accompanied with a general sensation of ease, sound nightly rest, and an increase of appetite, set in, and lasted uninterruptedly for about a week, at the rate of four or five discharges a day; after this period it stopped, and, since then, the bowels have been regular to the best of my knowledge. In a case of a most malignant impetigo serpiginosa of the face, and gradually spreading over the neck and arms with a rapidity that seemed truly frightful, two globules of the three-hundredth potency of Arsenic effected a perfect cure in three days. A number of careful and unprejudiced observers have reported cures with the highest potencies; it is doubtful, however, whether lower attenuations would not have been just as effectual as the former; at any rate, the endeavor to make them the normal doses in homœopathic practice, seems to me a rash and reprehensible undertaking.

There are practitioners who would fain make their patients believe, that the highest potencies constitute a species of homœopathy of a higher order. This is all fudge and flummery. The truth is that, in many respects, the highest potencies constitute one of the delusions of modern practice.

This is an appropriate opportunity of alluding to an erroneous impression that prevails among a certain portion of the public, namely: that the smallness of a dose constitutes its homœopathicity to a given case of disease. It has been shown in the foregoing pages that a medicine is only homœopathic to a disease when it is capable of reproducing, in the healthy organism, a disturbance that shall correspond in all its essential features and phenomena to the natural disease. The size of the dose does not affect the principle, but the principle determines more or less the size of the dose. It stands to reason that a homœopathic agent which is not given for the purpose of causing a revulsion in the system, but which acts directly upon the disease, in no other way than by gradually removing it and substituting in its stead a state of health, should be administered in a much smaller quantity than an allœopathic dose of medicine which is professedly given for revulsive ends. In regard to the size of the dose, homœopathic physicians sometimes resort to a disingenuous mode of reasoning. To their alloeopathic opponents they say that the size of the dose has nothing to do with the homœopathic law, and that an infinitesimal dose of an alloeopathically-administered mercurial preparation would not be any more a homœopathic dose than a hundred grains of the crude drug. And yet, the very men who employ this sort of argumentation, will turn round against such of their brethren as habitually use the lower attenuations or give larger quantities of medicine than themselves, and will endeavor to discredit them with the homœopathic public on the plea that they are no homœopathic physicians. They would fain make the world believe that they are Hahnemann's on a small scale; but they are not far above the followers of another great man, Wallenstein, of whom the corporal in Schiller's magnificent drama of that name, thus speaks to a recent recruit: "They walk, and spit, and clear their throats as he does, but the spirit, the mind are wanting."

It seems scarcely necessary to remark that, whatever dose may be employed in the treatment of disease, it should always be given within strictly conservative limits. The tincture of Nux Vomica affects the organism more powerfully than that of Euphrasia, and, all things being equal, should be given in smaller quantities than the latter; so should Arsenic be given in smaller quantities than Calcarea. This, however, only applies to the lowest preparations; in the higher attenuations the poisonous powers of the drugs disappear so completely, that all differences in the material size of the doses, depend exclusively upon the curative relation of the medicine to the disease. We will here remark in passing that one or two drops of the liquid attenuations, or even one half, fourth or sixteenth part of a drop; a few globules, or a grain or half a grain of the trituration, constitute the size of a dose.

IV. Repetition of the Dose.

Little need be said on this subject. In the earlier period of his practice, Hahnemann was in the habit of administering one dose only, and watching its effects for days, weeks, and even months, until the action of the drug seemed completely exhausted. More recently this course has been abandoned by most homœopathic physicians, and the medicines are given more frequently; a dose of the lower preparations may be repeated from every five or ten minutes, according to the requirements of the case, or the receptivity of the patient's organism, to every hour, or every two, three, four, six or twelve hours; the higher preparations should be repeated less frequently, every day, every two or three days, or should even be given once a week only. In the previous chapter, the cases where the lower and higher attenuations are to be used respectively, have been indicated. It is needless to repeat here what has been fully stated elsewhere.

This is a suitable opportunity of warning the student and the beginning practitioner of homœopathy against an error which is but too frequently committed by homœopathic physicians. I allude, not to the too frequent repetition of the same medicine, but to the unnecessary change of medicines in treating a case. There are practitioners who use ten, fifteen different medicines in a case where an intelligent physician, one who is thoroughly acquainted with his Materia Medica, would effect a cure in a much easier and more expeditious way by means of one or two remedies. This kind of treatment is either the result of ignorance or of a want of confidence in the efficacy of our remedies. There are diseases where it is necessary to employ different remedies, but there is scarcely a disease, even the higher forms of typhus, which cannot be effectually controlled by at most three or four remedies. In many diseases, where the books advise the use of several remedies, a single remedy is frequently sufficient to a cure. Thus, in regard to inflammatory diseases, with or without local inflammations, we are advised to commence the treatment with Aconite, and to change this medicine for Bryonia, Belladonna, or some other remedy, as soon as the synocha has been transformed into a simple erethic fever. This is all wrong. If a medicine has produced a decided improvement in the symptoms; that is, if the symptoms remain the same, but are less intense, or if only some of them have disappeared, and the others remain with the same degree of intensity: the original medicine which caused this modification of the primitive group, should be continued for this reason, that such a modification of the original disease is not an evolution of a new group of symptoms, but simply a quantitative reduction of the former symptoms. Let us suppose a case of inflammatory rheumatism with a full and bounding pulse, high fever, pains in the joints and bones, swelling and inflammation of the joints or muscles. Of course, we should prescribe Aconite; and, after using three or four doses of this medicine, we will suppose that the fever has not only abated, but has been entirely subdued, the pains in the bones are less, and the inflammation is considerably reduced. This change in the symptoms does not constitute a new group requiring a different remedy; on the contrary, the same remedy is still indicated, and, if continued, perhaps in reduced quantity and at longer intervals, the remaining symptoms will speedily disappear. As a general rule, the books do not distinguish between a reduction of the original disease to a lesser degree of intensity, and the evolution of a new or different group of symptoms, constituting a different phasis or stage of the original disease, and requiring a different treatment. In the higher forms of typhus, for instance, groups of symptoms will sometimes develope themselves in a series which are qualitatively, not quantitatively, distinct from each other, and which, therefore, require to be treated with different remedies.

As there is a reduction of the original symptoms to a lesser degree of intensity, so there may be an increase of these symptoms to a higher degree of intensity requiring a change in the dose, not the medicine.

Supposing a patient had undergone alloeopathic treatment for phlegmonous inflammation, or for such a species of inflammation as we would prescribe Aconite for in our practice, Aconite would still be indicated as corresponding with the original disease. The apparent change which this treatment might have effected in the symptoms, would not constitute a new group pathologically distinct from the original group; it would simply be the original disease elevated to a higher, or depressed to a lower degree of intensity, but absolutely identical in a pathological point of view with the former condition, and only quantitatively different from it.

It is of the utmost importance that the student of homœopathy should have these facts impressed upon his mind. An incredible amount of injury is inflicted upon the sick by the random sort of prescribing that a great many practitioners resort to, and which, if universally practised, would be a death-blow to our art, and a disgrace to our profession.

V. On the alternate use of Medicines.

Homœopathic physicians do not combine any of their medicines into one, although they sometimes give two medicines in alternation, at suitable intervals.

Physicians who treat disease in accordance with proper principles, and with a full knowledge of the nature of the symptoms, will scarcely ever deem it necessary to prescribe two different remedies at one and the same time. The custom of alternating two different remedies, has had its origin in a one-sided view of the nature of disease. If the symptoms of a disease were viewed as they ought to be, and as Hahnemann viewed them, (see Sect. 11, 14 and 15 of the Organon,) namely, as the phenomenal manifestations of an internal state, and if their pathological connection and dependance upon each other were properly known, it would most probably never be necessary to prescribe two remedies at the same time. It is only when symptoms are viewed superficially, without reference to their internal unity, that it seems as though they were disconnected, and required more than one remedy at a time. The common method of selecting a remedy consists in taking a record of the symptoms according to a certain plan, and then selecting from among the remedies that constitute our Materia Medica, one that has as nearly as possible the same symptoms, and, if one remedy do not suffice, physicians will select another one besides, in order to be sure that the symptoms of the disease are, as they term it, "covered" by the remedies. This mode of selecting a remedy, refers exclusively to the subjective symptoms, or the individual sensations of pain which are experienced by the patient; it does not take cognisance of the pathological state, of which these subjective sensations of pain are the mere external characteristics.

Cases may, perhaps, arise where the alternate use of two different medicines may be desirable; but these cases are few, just as few as the cases of two different diseases co-existing in the organism with all their characteristic symptoms distinctly and unmistakeably developed to the observing understanding. If we consider that every drug corresponds to a distinct pathological state, essentially differing from any other, we can only logically resort to the alternate use of two different medicines on condition that we should have to act upon two distinct pathological states, existing at one and the same time in the same organism. It has been abundantly shown in previous paragraphs, that such a combination is of very rare occurrence, and that the necessity for the alternate use of two different medicines can, therefore, only present itself as an exceptional mode of practice. The books present a great display of remedies that may be used in alternation, or in a certain order of succession. Such doctrines are generally a tissue of flimsy sophisms. The selection of a remedy under any circumstances depends upon the actually existing morbid state. In so far as it is positively known that certain morbid states succeed each other as invariably as night and day, the remedies which correspond to these states, likewise succeed each other with the same order and regularity. This point can only be settled by positive experience, not by speculative theory.

APPLICATION OF THESE GENERAL DOCTRINES TO THE TREATMENT OF DISEASE, AS TAUGHT BY HAHNEMANN.

The doctrines which have been developed so far, constitute the leading features of homœopathy. The application of these general principles to the treatment of disease is minutely taught in the Organon and in the first volume of the Chronic Diseases. The practical doctrines which the student of homœopathy will find expounded in these writings, refer to the following subjects:—

1. Treatment of acute and chronic diseases, including acute, epidemic and sporadic miasms.
2. Treatment of intermittent and alternating diseases.
3. Treatment of typical intermittent diseases.
4. Treatment of intermittent fevers.
5. Treatment of mental diseases.
6. Application of animal magnetism to the treatment of disease.
7. Regimen to be pursued by those who are under homœopathic treatment.

Those who are anxious to become acquainted with

Hahnemann's particular doctrines concerning these various subjects, are referred to the Organon, sections 72, 73, 74, 77, 78, 82, 84, 100, 204, 210, 231, 233, 235, 259, 262, and 293. In comparing the rules which Hahnemann here lays down for the treatment of the above mentioned classes of diseases, with the method of treatment which now prevails among homœopathic practitioners, it will be found that Hahnemann's suggestions and positive teachings are deviated from in almost every particular. And yet, to the attentive reader these teachings will appear full of wisdom, and characterized by a deep love and reverence for the Creator's masterpiece, the human organism. How anxiously Hahnemann avoids any interference, by the violent action of drugs, with the marvellous operations of its divine mechanism! With what deep and religious devotion he betakes himself to the task of dicovering the precise wants of the sick, and applying such remedies as by their prompt and pleasant action, will win the willing confidence of the patient! Under Hahnemann's guidance, the remedial agent indeed becomes a gentle friend, a loving restorer of health, and, for the first time since the creation of man, the healing art has been true to its high and noble mission, and, instead of *inflicting* pain, has kindly and permanently *relieved* it.

An elaborate statement of Hahnemann's original rules of practice could not be furnished without transcribing them in their totality. The principal features of these rules are—

1. The smallness of the dose, generally one or two globules of the thirtieth potency.

2. Careful avoidance of unnecessary repetitions of the dose; after having given the first dose, the physician is not to give a second one, until he has convinced himself by the most careful observation that one dose is not sufficient to make an impression upon the disease, and that the same medicine is still indicated by the symptoms.

3. No change of medicine unless required by a change in the perceptible symptoms of the disease.

4. Administration of the remedy by olfaction in a large number of cases.

5. Strict adherence to the diet recommended by Hahnemann.

6. Administration of only one simple medicine at a time. Hahnemann was decidedly hostile to all compounding of drugs, and to the alternate use of two or more drugs, which is almost constantly indulged in even by the strictest purists, and which can only be entirely avoided by those who believe in the specific relation of medicines to diseases. In section 272 of the Organon, Hahnemann uses this emphatic language in reference to this matter: "In no instance is it requisite to employ more than one simple medicine at a time." And in a note to this paragraph he records his opposition to the horrible abuse which threatened to break in upon the Homœopathic School, even during his lifetime, in the following words, the meaning of which must seem perfectly clear and unmis-

takeable to every unprejudiced follower of the great teacher. "Experiments have been made by some homœopathists in cases where, imagining that one part of the symptoms of a disease required one remedy, and that another remedy was more suitable to another part, they have given both remedies at the same time, *or nearly so;* but I earnestly caution all my adherents against such a hazardous practice, which never will be necessary, though, in some instances, it may appear serviceable."

These wise teachings are disregarded by modern homœopaths, some of whom regularly prescribe three and even four medicines at a time in almost every case of sickness. Such practices would gradually lead us back to the worst abuses of polypharmacy, if the seed that Hahnemann has sown, were not endowed with the imperishable vitality of eternal truth, and were not destined to grow up to a tree of life, freighted with the blessings of a regenerated race.

HAHNEMANN'S VIEW OF ACUTE AND CHRONIC DISEASES.

One of the peculiar features of Hahnemann's doctrines is his view of acute and chronic diseases, of which it seems appropriate to furnish a brief synopsis in this place.

Section 72, of the Organon, Hahnemann teaches that, "the diseases of mankind resolve themselves into two classes. The first are rapid operations of the vital power departed from its natural condition, which terminate in a shorter or longer period of time, but are always of moderate duration. These are called *acute* diseases. The others, which are less distinct, and often almost imperceptible on their first appearance, seize upon the organism,. each according to its own peculiar manner, and, by degrees, remove it so far from a state of health, that the vital power is only able to offer a fruitless resistance, and is compelled to allow these diseases to grow until, in the end, they destroy the organism. This second class of diseases is known by the appellation of *chronic* diseases; they are produced by infection from a chronic miasm."

Hahnemann classes acute diseases under two distinct heads. The first constitutes isolated cases of sickness, and arises from some pernicious cause to which patients have been exposed, such as excess in eating or drinking, starvation, violent physical influences, cold, heat, fatigue, etc., or violent emotions. The second kind arises from meteoric or telluric influences; it develops itself in a number of individuals at one and the same time, in different localities, and is, on that account, termed *sporadic*. Sporadic diseases are termed *epidemic*, when they become contagious by acting upon close and compact masses of human beings. War, inundations, and famine, frequently give rise to these diseases, but they may likewise result from *acute miasms*, which always reappear under the same form; some of them attacking man only once in his life-time, such as small-pox, measles, whooping-cough, the scarlet fever of Sydenham, mumps, etc.; whereas others may attack repeatedly, such as the plague, yellow-fever, Asiatic cholera, etc.

All *chronic* diseases, which properly claim this appellation, arise from three miasms, *psora*, *syphilis*, and *sycosis*. The characteristic sign of the syphilitic miasm is the chancre, and that of the sycosic miasm a cauliflower-shaped excrescence. The psoric miasm is the most inveterate and most universal of all chronic miasms. "It is not," says Hahnemann, in Sect. 80 of the Organon, "until the whole organism is infected, that psora declares its huge internal chronic miasm by a cutaneous eruption (sometimes consisting only in a few pimples) that is peculiar to it, and accompanied by an insupportable titillation, a voluptuous itching, and a specific odor. This psora is the sole, true and fundamental cause that produces all the other countless forms of disease which, under the names of nervous debility, hysteria, hemicrania, hypochondriasis, insanity, melancholia, idiocy, madness, epilepsy, and spasms of all kinds, softening of the bones, or rickets, scoliasis and cyphosis, caries, cancer, fungus hæmotodes, disorganizations and adventitious growths of all kinds, gravel, gout, piles, jaundice and cyanosis dropsy, amenorrhœa, gastrorrhagia, epistaxis, hæmoptysis, hæmaturia, metrorrhagia, asthma, phthisis, impotence and sterility, deafness, cataract and amaurosis, paralysis, loss of sense, pains of every kind, etc., appear in our pathology as so many peculiar, distinct and independent diseases."

"The progress of this ancient miasm through millions of organisms, in the course of hundreds of generations, and the extraordinary degree of development which it has by these means acquired, explains, to a certain extent, why, at the present time, it appears under so many different forms, especially if we contemplate the multiplicity of circumstances that usually contribute to this great diversity of chronic affections, (secondary symptoms of psora,) besides the infinite variety of their individual constitution. It is, therefore, not surprising, that such different organisms, penetrated by the psoric miasm, and exposed to so many hurtful influences, external and internal, which often act upon them in a permanent manner, should also present such an incalculable number of diseases, changes and sufferings, as those which have, till the present time, been cited by pathologists as so many distinct diseases, which are described by them under a variety of particular names."

Hahnemann spent twelve years in ferreting out the true source of this incredible number of chronic affections, and discovering the principal remedies with which the different forms of this psoric hydra could be successfully combated. To these remedies he gave the name of *anti-psorics.* The effects of these remedies upon the healthy organism are contained in a number of volumes, constituting, together with the treatise on the Nature and Treatment of Chronic Diseases, the second half of Hahnemann's Materia Medica. Previous to the discovery of the anti-psoric remedies, the homœopathic treatment of chronic diseases was, according to Hahnemann, exceedingly imperfect, and often unsuccessful; the use of the anti-psorics renders this treatment much more satisfactory.

This is the doctrine. At first it was hailed with an outburst of delight, and with a perfectly child-like faith. Death had lost its sting, and disease had been effectually and triumphantly conquered. Well, experience has most signally failed to confirm these brilliant expectations. Patients will die under homœopathic treatment as well as under any other, and a large number of diseases remain unconquerable. We have not yet succeeded in curing cancer, phthisis, organic diseases of the viscera; we are scarcely more successful in removing cataract, amaurosis, deafness, than alloeopathic practitioners; a large number of eruptive and nervous diseases defy the efficacy of our treatment; piles, irritations of the spinal column, blennorrhœa of the lungs, bowels, nose, remain uncured in hundreds of cases under homœopathic treatment; in short, the acclamations of joy with which the advent of the anti-psoric remedies was hailed by the disciples of Hahnemann, have dwindled down to feeble echoes of the primitive hymns of praise, and, in many quarters, have even been superseded by a positive want of faith, arising from bitter and frequent disappointments.

There was a time when, to differ with Hahnemann,

was to be a renegade, a non-believer in the orthodox church of homœopathy. This time is no more, thanks to the noble efförts of such men as Griesselich, Rau, Trinks, Arnold, and a host of other manly and devoted reformers, who had the courage and the talent to elevate homœopathy beyond the narrow limits of a mere science of sensual symptoms, to the exalted rank of a rational and queenly truth, to which chemistry, anatomy, pathology and physiology became subordinate and obedient, but indispensable supporters.

In company with many other honest and enlightened practitioners, I have devoted years of earnest thought to Hahnemann's doctrine of psora, and I must say that, however brilliant it may appear to some, it does not strike me as founded in reason.

Was the psoric miasm inherent in man when he first came out of the hands of his Maker, or did this psoric miasm first develope itself in the course of time, long after the first generations had passed away? It is immaterial which of these views we adopt to prove the unsoundness of Hahnemann's doctrine, that the host of morbid conditions which he enumerates in the first volume of his Chronic Diseases, from page 67 to page 98, constitutes a series of secondary effects of the internal psoric miasm, the chief primary symptom of which is the itch-pustule. Even if this doctrine were true, it does not, by any means account for the first origin of the internal psoric miasm of which the itch-pustule constitutes the external vicarious manifestation. This original miasm must, according to Hahnemann's own doctrine, have existed in the human organism anteriorly to any external manifestation in the shape of the itch-pustule, tinea, tetter, or any form whatsoever, and the question then arises: How did it first develope itself? From what causes did it originally spring? Evidently not from the retrocession, by natural or artificial means, of its vicarious cutaneous symptom which had not as yet any existence. This miasm must either have formed one of the constituent principles of the human organism, when it was first moulded into form, and quickened into life by the Divine Creator, or else the miasm must have supervened at a later period, and in this case humanity must either have been infected with it by some evil genius, whom God allowed to consummate this work of destruction, that his own high ends might be furthered thereby, or else the miasm arose from man's universal deviation from the laws of harmonic life. Man cannot possibly enjoy perfect health until he has achieved a perfect adjustment or correspondence between material nature and the laws that regulate human life; and this perfect adjustment cannot possibly take place until the laws of harmonious life are known, and all the arrangements of man's social and sensual life are absolutely adapted to the primordial conditions of his nature. How can it be expected, for instance, that man should enjoy health, as long as he has it not in his power to regulate atmospheric influences, to establish a universal system of adequate ventilation, to introduce habits of cleanliness into every household, to procure for every human being a sufficient quantity of suitable raiment, of wholesome food, of refreshing and invigorating water, and of harmonious exercise of the universal organism by productive and attractive labor, and finally, to secure to every man, woman, and child, the perfect and constant enjoyment of all the legitimate affections of the soul, the spontaneous realization in action of all the true and essentially useful ideas of the mind, and a fulness of that deep and religious peace which unavoidably arises from the consciousness of living in the order of one's God-appointed destiny. Even if a number of men, or a majority of the race were living in these conditions of harmony, the development of a morbific miasm could not be avoided. A single foul spot in the best governed city, and among a perfectly healthy population, would be sufficient to generate disease, and decimate the population of an empire.

Here let us rest, and let us cease to speculate beyond those self-evident agencies through whose instrumentality disease first introduced itself into the world. Man was ignorant of the true laws of life; he ate improper food, he lived on roots and raw meat, or he ate enormous quantities of flesh, feasted on blood and fat, was exposed to the inclemencies of the weather, inhabited smoky, dark rooms, or even subterraneous dens, deprived of fresh air, without cleanliness, doomed to hard and enervating labor, and the fairest portion of the race changed to an abject, degrading bondage; men and beasts all huddled up together in the same gloomy hut; wallowing in the same mire; inhaling the same death-harboring stenches; bellowing, roaring, barking, swearing together, in the same horrible discord; it is to such influences that we must trace the first immediate or proximate causes of disease, and not to the suppression of the cutaneous symptom of a miasm that was itself a result of man's primitive deviation from the divine laws of life. If chronic diseases are decreasing in number and intensity, it is not so much owing to the curative influence of anti-psoric medicines as to improved habits of diet, to a better system of general hygiene, ventilation, to a more harmonious exercise of the body, to the enjoyment of better food and raiment by the masses of the population, and to the universal spread of cleanliness and comfort. The strictness with which all the hygienic and atmospheric circumstances of the patient, are regulated by homœopathic practitioners, is one of the leading conditions of their successful treatment of chronic diseases; and what medicines may be required to achieve the cure, are just as often selected from among our common remedies, as from the so-called anti-psorics.

PART II.

CRITICAL REVIEW

OF THE

DOCTRINES OF HOMŒOPATHY,

AS APPARENTLY TAUGHT IN THE ORGANON,

AND AS

COMMONLY UNDERSTOOD BY THOSE WHO CLAIM TO BE THE ORTHODOX FOLLOWERS OF HAHNEMANN.

PART II.

It is as much from a sense of duty as from a desire to benefit our fellow-beings, that we should assume the position of reformers of medicine generally, and of the homœopathic practice in particular. The old system of medicine, vulgarly known under the name of allœopathy, has been sufficiently criticized by Hahnemann, and even by its own adherents, to permit me to leave it to its natural fate, which, I trust, it will share in common with every other system of medicine, viz: to pass through a series of successive modifications and a gradual contraction of its proportions, until the germs of disease shall either have been extirpated from the world, or, at any rate, shall have become so few and feeble, that a well regulated diet, proper exercise, an harmonious system of education, the internal and external use of cold water, and an abundance of pure and fresh air, shall be amply sufficient to remove the trifling disturbances which then may take place in the functions of the animal organism. My present object is to fulfil the solemn task of pointing out to all enlightened friends of medical progress the truths as well as the fallacies of the old-fashioned practice of homœopathy, and elevating its character, in the eyes of all truth-loving and intelligent men, both as a science and an art.

The fundamental principle upon which the homœopathic system rests, and in accordance with which the cures which are performed by homœopathic physicians, are supposed to be achieved, is the well known formula, "*similia similibus curantur*," the English of which is fitly rendered by "*like cures like.*" The meaning of this formula is that, in order to cure a disease, we have to prescribe a medicine which, if taken in sufficiently large quantities by a healthy person, will produce, in the healthy organism, a train of symptoms exactly similar to the symptoms of the natural disease which we are called upon to cure. Hence, to cure a sick headache, we have to prescribe a medicine that will produce an exactly similar headache in a healthy person. Or, to cure an inflammation of the lungs, we have to give a medicine that will cause an exactly similar disturbance of the pulmonary apparatus in a healthy person. Or, to cure a case of neuralgia, we have to administer a drug capable of affecting the healthy organism in an exactly similar manner. And so with all other diseases, of whatever organ, tissue or part of the body. To prescribe a medicine in accordance with the principle, "*like cures like,*" it is evident that we have, in the first place, to be acquainted with a medicine that shall be capable of developing, in the healthy organism, all the symptoms of the natural disease. Indeed, we cannot employ the medicine until we have first tried it on a number of healthy persons; in other words, a number of healthy persons of both sexes, and of various ages, temperaments and constitutions, must have swallowed a sufficient portion of the original drug to develope all the various effects which it is capable of producing in the human organism. As long as these effects are not exactly known, it is impossible that any homœopathic physician should, under any circumstances, be able to administer one of his drugs in strict conformity with his principle of "*similia similibus*," or "like cures like." Indeed, in order to secure a perfectly true application of this formula to the treatment of diseases, it would, in the first place, seem necessary that, before we can be perfectly sure of the curative operations of a drug in any given case, the patient should have tried, or, according to the technical phrase of homœopathists, "*proved*" this drug upon himself, while in a state of perfect health; for no two persons are ever affected alike by the same drug; nor does the same disease ever develope exactly the same symptoms in any two cases; the careful observer will perceive differences, were they ever so minute, but still differences arising from differences of temperament and constitution, or from various idiosyncrasies which, in the great society of men, constitute every human being an individual perfectly distinct from all other individuals of the same family. This mode of reasoning shows that the homœopathic law of "like cures like," is, in reality, a dogmatic abstraction, and that its strict or literal application in the treatment of disease, is simply impossible. For, it cannot be expected that every person who may possibly be sick once in his lifetime, should previously poison himself with every drug that is used in medical practice, in order to find out what diseases it might possibly cure in his own case; nor can it even be expected that a sufficient number of devoted men should be found willing to swallow sufficiently large portions of a poisonous substance, and to persevere in this practice for a sufficient length of time, in order to obtain even a tolerable certainty of the varied effects of the drug upon the animal economy, and a sufficiently correct representation of the various diseases to which these effects are similar, and which the drug, in accordance with the homœopathic law of similarity is, therefore, supposed capable of curing. There are many diseases which it would be absolutely impossible to reproduce in the human organism by artificial means. Of this number are the various cutaneous eruptions, eruptive fevers, chronic hereditary taints and organic diseases, such as enlargements of organs, arthritic deposits, effusions into the cavities of the brain, chest, abdomen; glandular indurations, schirrous disorganizations, consumptive conditions, malformations. A great many of these diseases can be, and have been, cured, and yet no prover has ever yet succeeded in developing similar diseases by mere drugs; indeed, howsoever far a single man's devotion to science may, now and then, be carried, it is not probable that a number of men will deliberately consent to poison themselves systematically for a long time, until their constitutions shall have become so thoroughly impregnated with the poisonous drug that the external or internal disorganizations which the provers had finally succeeded in developing in their organisms, could no longer be removed by an antidotal treatment, and must, therefore, remain as permanent alterations of their health, with their usefulness impaired and their peace of mind disturbed by a course of experimentation which, after all, may neither have been the most judicious, nor, indeed, the right way of attaining scientific precision in the treatment of disease.

But it is not merely organic diseases that are beyond the reach of a strict application of the homœopathic law; there is scarcely any known disease the form of which is reproduced with sufficient completeness and correctness in the provings of the homœopathic Materia Medica, to enable a practitioner to select a remedy for a given disease in accordance with the known symptoms of the drug. Take, for instance, that vast class of diseases which pathologists term "fevers." For the common inflammatory fever characterized by a full and bounding pulse, heat and dryness of the skin, preceded by, or mingled with, cold creepings or chills; and further characterized by such accessory symptoms as thirst, coated tongue, headache, nausea or vomiting, diarrhœa or constipation, and a variety of other symptoms, homœopathic physicians prescribe the tincture of Aconite either in its concentrated or attenuated form; and this preparation is undoubtedly the true remedy for this disease, and cures it specifically much better than any other known or probably unknown drug. But what symptoms, among the provings of Aconite, point so evidently and unmistakeably to this drug as the most appropriate remedy for fever, that no other medicine could possibly be thought of in preference to Aconite? And what now shall we say of the literal homœopathicity of Aconite to the various acute inflammations which homœopathic physicians cure with this drug? With Aconite they cure an inflammation of the lungs, save those cases where some other drug may be required. With Aconite they cure acute pleurisy, acute ophthalmia, an acute inflammation of the bowels, of the liver, or of almost any organ and tissue in the body. But what symptoms, among the known provings of Aconite, point to this drug as the true remedy for orchitis, for acute hepatitis, or for pneumonia? I do not say that there is any better remedy for these diseases; I simply ask, what are the therapeutic indications, among the known physiological effects of Aconite, which justify a homœopathic practitioner to prescribe it as the first and best remedy for acute inflammations of glandular organs, of the muscular tissue, of the eye, ear, rectum, and so forth? I say that these indications do not exist, and that the use of Aconite, in these affections, is either based upon empirical routine, or else upon grounds which the literal formula "*similia similibus*" cannot legitimately claim as its own. No enlightened practitioner will undertake to find, among the provings of Aconite, a group of symptoms which shall be an exact and unmistakeable representation of ophthalmia, pneumonia, hepatitis, orchitis, gastritis, dysentery, etc., or of any of the acute gastric, bilious or rheumatic fevers for which Aconite is prescribed by every homœopathic physician.

My literary labors in the field of homœopathy have enabled me to become tolerably well acquainted with both the truths and the fallacies of the huge and inattractive fabric of our provings; and the result of my long-continued, earnest and conscientious studies, concerning the adaptation of the homœopathic law of similarity to the cure of disease, so far as this similarity is based upon an actually known resemblance between the symptoms of the drug and those of the disease, is this discouraging conclusion, that the homœopathic law of "like cures like," is only an *apparent* truth, and, therefore, in many cases, without any practical value. The cases of cure where the strikingly favourable results of the treatment are evidently to be traced to an exact resemblance between the natural action of the drug and the phenomena of the disease, simply tend to render the absence of this resemblance in other cases, so much more evident and striking, and to confirm every unprejudiced practitioner of homœopathy in the belief, that all his decidedly brilliant and unmistakeable cures depend upon a law which, if not superior to the mere law of external similarity, implies such a comprehension and application thereof as has not yet prevailed among a majority of our physicians.

But it is not merely the non-existence of a true similarity between the known symptoms of our drugs and those of the disease, that renders the homœopathic law illusory, if understood in a purely external or literal sense; the illusory character of this law is demonstrable to common sense by a pure process of reasoning based upon the general and universally-admitted facts of nature.

According to Hahnemann's mode of understanding the term "similarity," and applying his formula "*similia similibus*" to the treatment of disease, a physician has to proceed in this manner: All the symptoms that a patient complains of, the various sensations of pain that he experiences, the various eruptions, pimples, blotches, tubercles, tumors, etc., which are seen upon the skin; the color, smell, consistence and frequency of the urinary and alvine evacuations; the abnormal phenomena of the nervous system generally; the symptoms occurring during sleep, such as dreams, startings of the limbs or body, etc.; the period of the day when the pain is felt, the side of the body where it is felt, the conditions and situations in which it is excited, aggravated or diminished; all these symptoms have to be recorded with the most perfect minuteness on a sheet of paper, commencing at the head and ending at the feet, after which a remedy has to be found in the Materia Medica which shall present the same array of symptoms, and, if one cannot be found which is exactly similar, then the next similar, and, for the remaining symptoms another remedy, so that the group of symptoms which the natural disease presents, is *covered*, as it is termed, in its totality, by the combined symptoms of the remedies employed in this case. Those who desire to be acquainted with Hahnemann's own teachings in reference to this matter, may consult his "*Organon of Homœopathic Medicine*," 3d American edition, from pages 143 to 154. They will there find it stated in substance that Hahnemann repudiates all classification of diseases, all physiological and pathological relation of the symptoms; that disease, according to him, consists merely in a certain numerical arrangement of its perceptible symptoms, and that a cure is effected by means of a drug which is known to have produced these very symptoms in a healthy person, when taken by the latter in a sufficient quantity and for a sufficient length of time. These external symptoms are, according to Hahnemann, all that we can ever know of disease; the internal connection of the symptoms, the internal states of the organism, of which these symptoms are merely the outward manifestations or perceptible signs, must for ever remain hidden from the searching reason. Hahnemann denounces in bitter and emphatic language all attempts to interpret the true meaning of the outward symptoms agreeably to the light of physiology and pathology; a pain is to him a mere pain, no matter what its pathological character may be; it may be more or less severe, more or less permanent, more or less screwing, boring, stinging, and the like; but whether it is a purely nervous pain, or whether indicative of inflammation, tuberculous disorganization, suppuration, or of any other morbid process, does not trouble him any; in his eagerness to do away with every vestige of the common science of medicine, he rejects not only the received nomenclature of diseases, but he discards even the morbid conditions for which this nomenclature was intended. In Hahnemann's system of Homœopathy there is no longer an inflammation of the brain, lungs, liver, kidneys or bladder; there is no longer such a condition as typhus, jaundice, rheumatism, paralysis; all these diseases have ceased to be definite functional disturbances of particular organs or tissues; according to Hahnemann's theory they are mere general derangements of the organism, of which the physician, moreover, ought to know and investigate only the most uninteresting and most insignificant portion, viz.: the outward signs or pains, such as the patient feels and describes them, or the eruptions and swellings, not as they really appear to the eye of the scientific observer, but to the untaught eye of the layman who distinguishes the eruption merely by its color, shape, or the accessory symptoms of itching, gnawing, burning and the like, but overlooks the relation it holds to the disordered condition of the bilious secretions, the capillary circulation or the absorbent system. Hahnemann enjoins the most perfect indifference regarding the internal relation of the symptoms of the disease; if a patient complains of sour stomach and fluttering of the heart, he does not care to enlighten either himself or the patient concerning the physiological unity of these symptoms. Away, says Hahnemann, with your doctrines of hysteria or spinal irritation. Here is a patient whose extremities are weak, numb, cold or burning; his chest feels oppressed, the beats of his heart are irregular, his digestive functions are impaired, he spits up his food, or every thing he takes into his stomach, turns sour; the bowels are deranged, at times loose, at others exceedingly confined, or they feel sore, and severe colicky pains or cramps are frequently experienced in the bowels. The soreness, weakness and lameness of the back, and the tenderness of the spinal column to contact or pressure, point to the spine as the true seat of the disease and the locality against which our remedial efforts should be principally directed. But Hahnemann stigmatizes all attempts to obtain a rational perception of the internal unity of the sensual symptoms, as preposterous; he condemns every effort to give our treatment a precise, positive, well-sustained direction, and to account to ourselves, to the satisfaction of our reason, for the favorable or unfavorable changes which are taking place in the condition of the patient. Hahnemann was undoubtedly right in combating the system which seems to have prevailed almost exclusively before he introduced his measures of reform. This system consisted in prescribing a set list of remedies for names of diseases. The Doctor, after examining his patient, pronounced the case a case of dropsy; and thereupon he consulted his repertory, or, from his memory, copied the prescriptions which were recommended for this disease. Either the patient got well, or else he died; but, if he did die, he died *secundum artem*, and this was the doctor's consolation and his justification before the world. It was Hahnemann's mission to break this charm, and it must be confessed that he proved a terrible disturber of the self-complacent dogmatism which had enchained the minds of physicians for so many centuries, and had rendered the science of medicine inaccessible to all rational reforms. Hahnemann promulgated, and insisted upon, the interesting truth that every case of disease constitutes a distinct and characteristic deviation from the normal condition of the organism; that its phenomena or symptoms should be carefully observed and recorded, and that the case should be treated upon its own merits, not as a rheumatic, nervous, or gastric disease, but as a disturbance of the organism characterized by certain observable outward signs or symptoms. This process of individualizing the phenomena of disease, was undoubtedly a progress over the old-fashioned method of prescribing, in regular order, a set of medicines for mere names of diseases; but, in the hands of Hahnemann, this process of individualization became as fatiguingly and pedantically minute, as the dogmatic generalizations of the old School had been destructive of the individual characteristics of disease. His directions to the physician for discovering and tracing out an image of the disease, as it is termed by Hahnemann; or, in other words, for taking a record of the totality of the perceptible symptoms, constitute such a minute, and, at the same time, such an arbitrary interrogatory, that there is scarcely any homœopathic physician in our time who conforms to it in his intercourse with his patients. Indeed, it is impossible, in thousands of cases, to subject patients to a rigid cross-examination of several hours' duration, as every follower of Hahnemann is obliged to do, if he means to be true to his master's teachings.

In the treatment of mental diseases it is frequently impossible to obtain from the patient's own lips an intelligible account of his sufferings. Little children are likewise unable to relate their sensations of pain, oppression, anxiety. And how are we to become acquainted with the symptoms of patients laboring under a fit of apoplexy, or seized with tetanic convulsions, with the delirium of typhus, an acute hæmorrhage from the lungs, or some other acute disorder where a total or partial loss of consciousness incapacitates the patient from giving an account of his condition? In many cases of disease, physical weakness, the acuteness of the pain, or the peculiar seat of the disease, would render a long and detailed examination of the patient either impossible or dangerous. It would be cruel to subject a patient seized with acute asthma, or with the oppressive anguish of pericarditis, to a cross-examination after the Hahnemannean fashion. In many other cases it would be dangerous to waste much time on a long examination of the so-called subjective symptoms. What physician who is sent for in the middle of the night to arrest an hæmorrhage from the lungs or uterus, will stand idly by, and, while the life-pulse of his patient is ebbing feebler and feebler, amuse himself with taking a record of all the principal and accessory symptoms of the case? And so in a case of impending paralysis. What more positive indication does the physician require in such a case than the state of the pulse? Does not the labored and slow beating at the wrist point in unmistakeable language to the necessity of an immediate stimulation of the heart's action? The allœopathic physician seeks to attain this result by venesection and revulsive means, the homœopathic by the exhibition of suitable internal agents; but whether allœopathic or homœopathic, what need is there of any protracted examination?

If the healing art embody a principle of scientific truth, the physician will at once perceive the character and extent of the danger, and be able to avert it, if this be at all possible, by a definite, certain, and safe course of medication. And, if Hahnemann's method of taking a record of all the perceptible phenomena of a disease, be the only true mode of diagnosing its essential nature, and determining our choice of a suitable remedial agent, what is to become of the brute creation? Are our valuable domestic animals to be abandoned to their fate when sickness overtakes them? Is veterinary surgery, this most interesting portion of the healing art, to be abolished? This will inevitably result from the Hahnemannean formula, "like cures like," unless the Creator should consent, for the special benefit of homœopathists, to endow the brutes with rationality and such other means of communication as may be required for a satisfactory statement of their pains and derangements.

The objections which I have thus far offered against the law of similarity, as propounded by Hahnemann, it strikes me, are of a very grave character, and appear to me unanswerable. Nor are they the only ones. The present homœopathic Materia Medica is composed of some three hundred drugs, all of which have been proved, more or less fully, on healthy persons. I shall hereafter have occasion to show that these provings are exceedingly unreliable and illusory. But, the homœopathist who has incorporated these provings in his Materia Medica, is of course disposed, and indeed, bound to be guided by his drug-symptoms in the selection of a remedy for some particular case of disease. Now let us open the ponderous volumes of the homœopathic Materia Medica, and we shall find that the symptoms of many homœopathic drugs are so nearly alike, that it is absolutely impossible to select a remedy with any thing like certainty, for any disease you may name. Let a physician who is not acquainted with the established routine-practice of homœopathy, undertake to cure a headache with the means offered him in his Materia Medica. A simple headache seems to be a very trifling affection, which ought easily to be cured, if there be any truth in medicine. Years of practice and observation have gradually developed a certain routine-practice out of the crude ingredients of the homœopathic Materia Medica, and a physician who is somewhat acquainted with the established routine, will at once associate a headache with a certain group of drugs, such as Aconite, Belladonna, Mercurius, Nux vomica, Pulsatilla, Arsenic, and so forth. And he will not have any great trouble in deciding in favor of one or the other of these drugs; if one should fail, he can easily try another; the number is not so very extensive, and, by the time two or three members of the group have been tried, the headache has got well any how, and probably would have got well without the interference of the physician. But let a physician who has no sort of knowledge of the customary routine-practice of the homœopathic brotherhood, and who has to rely exclusively on his knowledge of the Materia Medica, undertake to treat this headache. What remedy is he going to prescribe? By what signs is he to discriminate between Aconite and Belladonna, Mercurius or Nux, Arsenic or Pulsatilla? How is he, satisfactorily to his own conscience, to decide in favor of any one particular drug, among the several hundred from among which he has to select one, and either hit the right remedy, or else fail of affording relief to his patient? All these drugs have a variety of headache-symptoms, and, unfortunately, most of these symptoms are so nearly alike, that, with a few exceptions, it would be impossible to divine the name of the drug from the symptoms which are recorded as belonging to it in the Materia Medica. Take any thirty or forty of the leading drugs, Platina, Arsenic, Calcarea, Sulphur, Alumina, Natrum muriaticum, etc., and you will find nearly the same pains recorded among the headache-symptoms, be they shooting, lancing, jerking, twisting, burning, stinging, screwing, constrictive, compressive, aching or any other kinds of pain. And if, after comparing all these different drugs with each other with the most faithful perseverance, a physician finally decides in favor of a certain remedy, and administers it in the positive expectation of relieving his patient; how bitter must be his disappointment, if no favorable change follows the exhibition of his drug? What is he to do now? He had made every effort to select his remedy in accordance with the perceptible symptoms of the case; he feels unable to discover a greater degree of similarity between the symptoms of the disease, and those of any other drug besides the one he had used; nothing now remains for him than blind empiricism. His sheet-anchor having failed him, he now has to try one drug and then another, until he finally, by some lucky chance, either hits on the right remedy, or until, which is much more probable, and is, indeed, much more frequently the case, the disease has, in the meanwhile, run its course, and arrived at its natural termination. This is not an imaginary case, but it is the fate of every new convert to homœopathy, who undertakes to practise his art agreeably to the demands of the Organon. He soon finds out that he has to forsake the speculative paths of the master, and has to betake himself to some kind of routine-practice in order to satisfy his conscience, and afford relief to his confiding patients. The symptoms which we find recorded in the homœopathic Materia Medica as constituting the genuine effects of drugs upon the healthy organism, are too much alike to enable the practitioner to discriminate with scientific accuracy between the symptoms of one drug and those of another. This homogeneity of the symptoms not only runs through the symptoms of the head, but exists throughout the Materia Medica in the recorded symptoms of almost every part of the human body. The throat-symptoms, the symptoms of the chest, bowels, extremities, and those of the special senses, are, in most respects, so nearly alike, that those of one drug might easily be taken for the symptoms of another. What homœopathic physician would undertake to cure a case of constipation, or of the opposite state, diarrhœa, if he had no other therapeutic indications to depend upon than the abnormal conditions of the alvine evacuations, as recorded in the Materia Medica? The same drug is invariably a remedy for constipation and a remedy for diarrhœa, a remedy for strangury and a remedy for the opposite state, enuresis, a remedy for a loss of appetite, and for a ravenous desire for food, for excessive menstruation, and for retention of the menses. Opposite states, such as farsightedness and nearsightedness; emaciation and adiposis; sleeplessness and drowsiness; desire for, and aversion to food; excessive thirst, or loss of thirst; pale or flushed face; dryness of, or discharge of mucus from the nose, and a variety of other states, are almost invariably found among the symptoms of most of the important drugs in the homœopathic Materia Medica.

To be sure, Hahnemann gets partially over the difficulty by claiming for some drugs the power of producing alternate effects, one series of effects to-day, and another series of opposite effects to-morrow. But such metaphysical speculations do not satisfy the impartial reason. Opposite effects never emanate from the same cause, and it is much more probable that, if a drug seemed to produce opposite effects at different periods, neither can be rightfully attributed to it. What has been the unavoidable consequence of this vagueness and sameness of the homœopathic Materia Medica? Simply this, that the Materia Medica is emphatically discarded by most physicians; very few consider it worth their while to study this frightful and incoherent agglomeration of ill-defined, vague and often unmeaning symptoms, and most physicians rely upon some practical manual or repertory to help them out in case of need. And, by this means, the practice of homœopathy has been reduced to a system of routine similar, in many respects, to the much abused, and severely condemned routine-practice of the Old School, with this difference, that homœopathic physicians prescribe set remedies for *symptoms*, whereas, in the Old School, medicines were prescribed for the collective appellations of diseases. Take a case of gastric fever. If the pulse be full, hard and bounding, and the skin hot and dry, the homœopathic physician will prescribe Aconite as the proper remedy for this condition ; but, if the bowels should, at the same time, be constipated, most physicians will consider themselves bound to alternate the Aconite with a few doses of Nux vomica or Bryonia, simply because they had learned from somebody, or read in some manual, that Nux and Bryonia are proper remedies for constipation, and that, on this account, the aforesaid case of gastric fever with constipation, would not be treated *secundum artem,* if the Aconite were not duly alternated with Nux or Bryonia. Not all physicians seem to understand that the constipation, in this case, is not a primary symptom, but a necessary result of the embarrassed or depressed condition of the capillary action, and that, if the capillary system be restored to its normal vigor and elasticity by specific remedial influences, the constipation will cease of itself. But, if the fever should happen to be accompanied with diarrhœa, then Pulsatilla would generally be substituted for Nux, for no other earthly reason than because Pulsatilla is recommended for diarrhœa as a symptom of gastric derangement. And, if the fever should be accompanied with vomiting of mucus or bile, the probability is that most physicians would alternate the Aconite with a few doses of Ipecacuanha, simply because they happen to know that this drug is recommended for vomiting. But, if the vomiting should be moreover complicated with burning in the pit of the stomach, Arsenic would undoubtedly take the place of Ipecacuanha, because it is an invariable rule with most homœopathic physicians to prescribe the former drug for "burning." Now, it will be readily admitted by all intelligent practitioners of the homœopathic healing art, that this method of prescribing remedies for mere symptoms, is not, by any means, satisfactory to the scientific reason, and that, if it were carried to its ultimate boundaries, homœopathy would indeed become, in the words of the illustrious Hufeland, "the grave of medicine."

These remarks lead me to another grave and vital objection to the mode in which homœopathy is practised by some physicians, an objection which is founded on the incompleteness and unreliableness of the materials out of which the homœopathic Materia Medica is composed. Let us examine this subject a little more closely, and it will at once become apparent that the material basis of homœopathy, viz., the provings or drug-symptoms which make up the homœopathic Materia Medica, so far from constituting a series of incontrovertible facts, is, on the contrary, liable to the grave and well-founded charge of being, in a great measure, a tissue of fallacies, illusions, misapprehensions, absurdities, and childish observations.

Previous to Hahnemann, regular provings of drugs upon the healthy, were not deemed necessary to secure a perfect adaptation of the remedial agent to the disease. The pharmacodynamic properties of drugs were generally known only from some accidental cases of poisoning, or from the effects produced by an excessive dose of the drug, which constituted, after all, a peculiar species of legalised poisoning. One drug was simply known as an emetic, more or less mild or severe in its operations, but still only as an emetic; another drug as a febrifuge; another as a sudorific; another as a diuretic; another again as a rubefacient; another as an antiphlogistic; and these unsatisfactory generalizations led to, and confirmed the exceedingly speculative practice of former times. The healing art, it strikes me, consisted simply of the few very general and very vague operations of bleeding, sweating, purging, vomiting, salivating, stupefying, stimulating, or blistering the patient; and the scorching satire which the keen genius of Molière has inflicted upon the dogmatism and the self-sufficient pride of the profession, in his "MALADE IMAGINAIRE;" howsoever humiliating this imperishable monument of wit and comedy may appear to all superficial and truth-dreading followers of Æsculapius, must, nevertheless, be received as a permanent protest of the insulted sense and the wounded sensibilities of humanity against the barbarous empiricism which had been enthroned in the schools as the goddess of medical truth, and was worshipped by an infatuated and ignorant multitude as heaven's sublimest inspiration, and the prerogative of unapproachable and mysterious genius. It is true, a great many, and, indeed, all the noble spirits of the profession, had recorded their condemnation of the blind empiricism and sweeping generalizations of their art. Boerhaave, Sydenham, Huxham, Hoffmann, Girtanner, Haller, had expressed their dissatisfaction with the uncertainties of medicine and and the fanciful theories of her professors; but no positive and radical reforms had ever been proposed by any of these writers, and it must be admitted, that the first signal revolution in the principles and practice of medicine, whatever value may otherwise be attached to it by its friends or opponents, dates from the period when Hahnemann proclaimed the doctrine, that a cure can only be effected by means of drugs which are capable of producing, in the healthy organism, a train of symptoms exactly similar to those of the natural disease.

This doctrine opened an entirely new field to the observing reason. Facts which had hitherto been overlooked as unimportant and unessential, had to be investigated with the minutest care; it was no longer sufficient to know that the patient suffered pain, but the sensually-perceptible character of the pain had to be ascertained, whether it was a boring, screwing, lancinating, burning, stinging, twitching, jerking or any other kind of pain; it was no longer sufficient to be told that the patient complained of a stitch, but the direction, quality and size of the stitch had to be known, whether it was from within outwards, or from without inwards, from above downwards or from below upwards, whether it was a slow or a rapid, a tearing or a boring stitch, or whether it was striking through the space of an inch, a foot or the whole body. The new doctrine being, that the totality of the symptoms constitutes the disease, in a therapeutic point of view at least; and that the disease is cured internally when all the symptoms are extinguished, (see Hahnemann's Organon, pages 96–98:) it followed, as a matter of course, that an exact knowledge of the symptoms was the first requisite towards a cure. Nor can there be any logical difference of opinion among the strict followers of Hahnemann regarding the question: What constitutes a symptom? Nothing can possibly come under the category of symptoms which is not a sensually-perceptible deviation from the normal condition of the organism. It must be a pain, an eruption, or some kind of a perceptible disturbance of the functions. The physiological relation of one pain to another; of a dyspeptic state of the stomach to irregularities of the heart's action; of an abnormal coloring of the skin or a dropsical condition of the cellular tissue to a diseased state of the liver; of paralysis or atrophy of the extremities to spinal disorganizations; of the general emaciation of a child and the tympanitic distention of its bowels to a scrofulous enlargement of the mesenteric glands; of an effusion into the cavity of the chest to some organic affection of the heart; all such purely intellectual perceptions of the patient's condition, are logically speaking, banished from the domain of the homœopathic healing art, and, if Hahnemann's formula be strictly and literally true, must be necessarily superseded by the new art of recording all the morbid sensations, or, indeed, all the sensations of the patient, with the most rigorous exactitude. No perceptible alteration of the functions is allowed to escape. With pen in hand, the Hahnemannian follower is obliged to note every perceptible irregularity in the organism from the head to the foot, every little spot or pimple, every twinge of pain, the character, duration, starting-point, or periodicity of the pain, its alternate appearance or disappearance in one or the other side of the body; the exact color, shape, consistence, smell and quantity of the alvine and urinary evacuations, and the manner in which they are expelled, together with all the accompanying sensations of urging, pressing, smarting, ease or embarrassment; the cutaneous sensations and appearances, such as itching, gnawing, stinging, creeping, every little pimple, blotch, spot, and the like; the various conditions observable during sleep, such as dreams, whether pleasant or unpleasant, and about what; startings of the body or limbs; the position of the body, whether the patient is inclined to sleep on his back or belly, on the right or left side, with his arms extended along the sides of the body, or lying crosswise on the chest, or stretched above the head; with the lower extremities drawn up or stretched out, closely joined or spread apart; and so through every known function of the organism; every possible indication of a disturbed equilibrium is recorded with the greatest care as an essential feature of what Hahnemann terms "the image of the disease;" inferences or purely intellectual perceptions are categorically excluded from this world of symptoms; the patient's sensations as described in his own language, sensations of constriction or compression, fulness or emptiness, distention or sinking, weakness or strength, all the various noises of buzzing, ringing, fluttering, roaring, cracking, hissing, humming, snapping, blowing, thundering, whizzing, seething; all the various sensations of itching, gnawing, jerking, burning, thumping, hammering, jumping, bounding, twitching, screwing, boring, stinging, shooting, cutting, pinching, griping, grasping, clutching, clawing, forcing, urging, pressing, tearing, boring, pushing, aching, crampy or spasmodic pains; every possible form of pain, and all the conditions and influences which have reference to the external character of the pain, such as locality, period of occurrence, periodicity and so forth; in one word, all visible or tangible signs of disease, all alterations of the functions whether perceptible externally to the senses or internally to the patient's own consciousness, constitute, in the professional logic of every strict homœopathist, the chief, and, indeed, the sole object of cure; all these external signs form the true image and constitute the only attainable knowledge of the disease; it is to a correct perception and a complete and accurate record of these signs that the physician should bend all his energies; all investigations of the actual condition of the nervous system during the occurrence of certain pains; all inquiries into the pathological state of the organs during the development of certain alterations of the functions, are henceforth condemned as useless, dangerous, and, indeed, impossible speculations of erratic minds; no true homœopathist will ever dare to lift the veil which hides the mysterious processes of nature from the gaze of mortal eye; give us symptoms, nothing but symptoms; this is all we need to know of the character and the actual existence of disease; let us remove the symptoms, and the patient is radically and permanently cured.

I believe that I have stated Hahnemann's doctrine fairly and explicitly; I think I have the ability and the desire to state it fairly; indeed, I am not conscious of having done it injustice. Considering the doctrine without prejudice, it must be admitted that its conclusions seem very plausible. What remains of the disease when all its perceptible phenomena have disappeared? If any thing does remain, it is certainly beyond the reach of observation, and is, therefore, inaccessible to the resources of the healing art. Whence, then, comes the bitter opposition which has been raised against Hahnemann's doctrine, not only by the vulgar herd of practitioners or laymen, for it seems to be their mission to oppose progress in every shape or form, but also by thousands of enlightened, impartial, truth-seeking and truth-loving members of the medical profession? Whence all the ridicule, all the sarcasms, all the persecutions, all the denunciations which Hahnemann and his disciples have had to encounter in every country, until this very day? Can it be possible that all this antagonism should spring from prejudice or unthinking hatred? Or may there not have been something essentially inconsistent, something essentially absurd in the doctrines themselves that has provoked all this hostility? Is Hahnemann's criticism, in all respects, just and philosophical? Does it not scatter the wheat with the chaff, and does that which is offered by him in the place of a time-honored and cherished faith, commend itself by its own beauty to the judgments of the enlightened friends of progress as a truth of a higher order, as a positive and permanent good, or simply as a negative, unsubstantial illusion, as a merely symbolic representation of a living and undeniable law which is yet to dawn upon our minds, and claim the homage of our hearts as its legitimate and eternal birthright? More than one bold and generous disciple of Hahnemann has dared to step out of the ranks, and to proclaim the fact that the deep and systematic opposition to homœopathy was based upon serious grounds; and they have never ceased, in earnest and eloquent appeals, to invite their brethren to a conscientious examination of their opinions, and their mode of carrying out their own conception of the homœopathic law. It must not be supposed that modern homœopathy is at all like the old-fashioned Hahnemannism. Most of the thinking minds of the homœopathic brotherhood had become dissatisfied with the original teachings of Hahnemann, and, under the leadership of such men as Rau, Griesselich, Trinks, they organized an opposition to the master, which has so completely changed the aspect of the Homœopathic School in Germany, at least,—and Germany is still a focus of all genuine reform in science, philosophy, and religion—that, so far from its being the grave of medicine, as it fairly threatened to become under the invasion of a mass of spurious symptoms and baseless theories, many of the homœopathic reviews and journals now published in Germany, England, and the United States, rank undoubtedly among the most valuable and philosophical contributions to medical literature.

The opposition to Hahnemann's doctrine arose, then, not so much from his own criticism of the existing doctrines of the Schools, as from the incompleteness and partial unsoundness of the system which he sought to force upon the profession, first by his unsparing criticism of the humoral pathology which was then in vogue, and secondly, by his reiterated and positive assurance that the homœopathic system, as taught by him, was the only true method of cure. Here was the chief point of difference between Hahnemann and his alloeopathic opponents, as well as his most distinguished disciples. Supposing we admit the correctness of his premises, that the removal of all the perceptible symptoms of a disease, constitutes a cure, does it then follow that we must necessarily accept the means which he proposes to effect this end, as the best, most rational, and most expeditious? It is not so much his original premises that were assailed, as the means which he proposes to remove the totality of the perceptible symptoms. His opponents say that these means are inadequate, and not, by any means, conformable to sound science. They say that his method of removing the symptoms reduces the healing art to the mechanical process of opposing a series of natural symptoms by its exact counterpart of drug-symptoms, without considering the essential or internal states of the organism of which the external or sensually-perceptible symptoms are mere phenomenal manifestations; and they assert furthermore, and certainly very justly, that this mechanical "COVERING," as it is termed, of one series of symptoms by another, will prove destructive of all true medical science, and will, in the end, destroy itself as one of the illusions of the infantile reason of humanity. Leaving for the present a close examination of the dazzling sophisms which this illusion embodies, with a view of resuming it by and by in its order, let us now look at the character of the means with which we are required to remove the symptoms of disease.

The disciples of Hahnemann, as well as most other physicians, cure diseases by means of drugs. The same drugs are mostly used in both the homœopathic and allœopathic Schools, although homœopathic physicians generally use a great many more drugs than their allœopathic opponents. To oppose a series of natural morbid symptoms by a similar series of drug-symptoms, the symptoms which a drug is capable of producing in the healthy organism, have not only to be known with perfect exactitude, but also in their totality. For, taking it for granted that the homœopathic formula "*similia similibus*" embodies the whole of therapeutic truth, how could this formula be applied to the treatment of disease unless all the symptoms of a drug were known? Twenty different drugs may all produce the same kind of a headache, or a headache so nearly alike that differences can hardly be said to exist. But a few characteristic differences may be discovered between the abdominal or thoracic symptoms, and it may be the accidental co-existence of one or more of these accidental differences in the natural morbid group, that may lead us to the selection of the true remedy from among this number. But, supposing these characteristic symptoms should be wanting either in the natural or artificial group, how then are we going to decide which of these twenty remedies will cure the headache? This will be found a hard matter, and, in truth, a sheer impossibility, as every beginner in homœopathy will soon discover to his great sorrow and disappointment. The natural group of symptoms is entirely beyond our control; the laws of life, and the influences by which they happen to be disturbed, are the determining causes of this group, and regulate it according to their own sovereign pleasure. But the artificial group, or the symptoms which the drug *contains*, as it were, within the recesses of its structural organization, and which it is the business of the prover to develope in a regular series, are more or less subject to his control, and their exact and complete evolution depends a good deal upon the arbitrament of his own judgment. For, he has to determine what substances in nature constitute, properly speaking, drugs, and from which of them such symptoms can be elicited as have a positive, unmistakeable therapeutic value; he has to determine whether those whom he desires to associate with himself in the business of proving, enjoy sufficient health and energy to bear the privations and fatigue which the trial of drugs involves, and are not exposed to influences that might impair the action of the drug or produce before the observing reason a train of adulterated or factitious symptoms; he has furthermore to determine in what quantities and order the drug which is to be proved, is to be taken, in order that its true physiological action may be fully and correctly developed; and finally, he has to watch the changes which are taking place in the organism during the trial of the drug, with persevering and discriminating attention, lest the drug should be credited for symptoms which are attributable to altogether different causes. The proving of drugs, therefore, involves a variety of eminent qualities of which the prover should be possessed, sound health, a discriminating judgment, a perfect absence of that species of vanity which delights in producing a vast array of symptoms at the expense of truth, and a noble enthusiasm which is not afraid of systematically inflicting pain and distress upon the bodily frame in the service of the holiest cause, the cause of suffering humanity. When Hahnemann first instituted systematic provings of drugs, he was surrounded by a band of devoted disciples who, under the leadership of their master, made it their sacred duty to sacrifice their comfort, and risk their very lives, in the noble endeavor of building up an authoritative, universally acknowledged Materia Medica upon the incontrovertible basis of positive experimentation. His Materia Medica Pura, with the magnificent provings of Aconite, Belladonna, Cinchona, Mercurius, Nux vomica, Ignatia, Pulsatilla, Ipecacuanha, and a number of other drugs, will be looked upon by the remotest posterity as a monument of careful and just observation of the physiological action of drugs upon the healthy organism. And more recently, the provings and re-provings of a body of Austrian homœopathic physicians deserve to be mentioned as instances of brilliant devotion in the cause of true medical science; or even, in our own country, the proving of the Lobelia cardinalis may be alluded to as an exquisitely true, although incomplete account of the therapeutic properties of this drug. Every symptom which these various provers have recorded as the positive effect of some drug, bears upon the face of it an undeniable expression of truth; and the complex of the symptoms of a drug reveals with unmistakeable accuracy its peculiar sphere of action as a therapeutic agent. All these symptoms were attained from the long-continued use of large quantities of the poison. In proving the Aconite for instance, Dr. Arneth, of Vienna, gradually increased the quantity of the drug, until he swallowed several hundred drops of the strong tincture at one time. Professor Zlatarovitch emptied a whole tumblerful of the tincture of Thuja occidentalis, after having tried lesser quantities for months. Dr. Müller proved the nitrate of silver with massive doses; others, the tinctures of Colocynth, Bryonia, Nux vomica, and so forth; all the medicines composing Hahnemann's Materia Medica Pura, and the additions thereto by his original co-provers, and which have been collected by Dr. Stapf into a separate volume, were experimented with in large doses of the tincture, in such a manner that these founders and apostles of the New School of medicine finally succeeded in obtaining a perfect picture of the pathogenesis of many drugs, and defining their positive spheres of action as remedial agents and the exact boundaries of their usefulness. But what shall we, what can we say of an enormous mass of symptoms which have been incorporated into the homœopathic Materia Medica by men who never knew how to distinguish between a fancy and an actual truth? In what way are the symptoms which are set down to the account of many drugs, which have been introduced since Hahnemann's demise, by a number of provers in different countries, distinguished from the numerous unpleasant sensations by which thousands of nervous systems are disturbed in the course of twenty-four hours, while merely exposed to the common influences of life, the anxieties and cares of business, the irritating action of atmospheric impurities, changes in the weather or wind, unwholesome food, excessive heat, dampness or rawness of the air, etc. Look at these pretended symptoms, and then ask yourselves the question whether a single one bears the test of a critical examination? Read the head-symptoms of a great many newly-added drugs; or the throat-symptoms, the chest-symptoms, or any other portion of the symptoms; dwell upon them with your mind's eye, and then see whether you do not arrive with me at the inevitable conclusion, that most of the recorded symptoms, if not all, are not likewise experienced by most men while engaged in the daily pursuits of life, and whether a most discouraging sameness in the symptoms does not expose the accuracy of the prover to legitimate suspicions? We frequently have such vague and unsatisfactory statements as pain in some part of the head, above the eyes, in the temples, forehead or occiput; or a beating, drawing or jerking in the head, or other insignificant sensations, all of which are stated in such a loose, flippant and superficial manner that they are not only perfectly valueless in practice, for the simple reason that nobody ever cares to apply to a physician for such trifling ailments; but that, at the same time, they cast a legitimate suspicion on those few symptoms, few and far between—*rari nantes in gurgite vasto,* scattered here and there over the immense abyss—which otherwise might seem to be attributable to the drug, but which, when discovered among such a mass of unreliable testimony, must be set down as the accidental results of some other disturbance of the organism, physical fatigue, constitutional debility, an unpleasant emotion, a cold, an indigestion or some such cause. A premium might safely be offered for every genuine drug symptom which may be found among many of our provings, and, if such a symptom should really exist, we are at a loss to determine to what disease it points in practice. It is pain in the head, pain in the throat, pain in the chest, pain in the shoulder, pain in the elbow, pain in the knee, pain in the back, pain here, pain there, pain all over, and this is a tolerably fair summing-up of the pathogenesis of many of our newly-added drugs. And new drugs are constantly being added, with frightful lists of symptoms. "*Quousque tandem abutere patientia nostra?*" How long will you still continue to abuse our patience? I address this Ciceronian interpellation to all those members of our profession who evince this terrible rage for new drugs and symptoms. Has not the homœopathic Materia Medica been transformed into a perfect Augean stable, that it will take not one, but a dozen Hercules to cleanse? A whole half of this incoherent mass of unmeaning symptoms might be expunged at one fell swoop, and all intelligent and conscientious members of our School would then have a chance to use the remaining half according to definite and unmistakeable indications. What homœopathic physician will be bold enough to assert that, in the present condition of his Materia Medica, he does not use two-thirds of his drugs empirically? And if he have not sufficient genius or independence to form to himself a routine practice out of the frightful mass of incoherent materials of which the present homœopathic Materia Medica is composed, I pity him with all my soul. Launched upon an ocean of doubts and uncertainties, he can scarcely ever know what remedy to prescribe; and he would lose seven-eighths of his patients, if kind nature did not come to his aid, and cured them for him.

It is interesting to inquire what makes a great many of our recent provings so unreliable in practice. This fact is easily accounted for. The homœopathic law of similarity led to an administration of the medicines totally different from that of the Old School. The medicines acting similarly to the disease, they had, of course, to be given in small quantities, lest the sympathy which naturally existed betwen the medicine and the disease, should give rise to a violent or even dangerous aggravation of the natural morbid symptoms. This, at any rate, was a natural supposition, and naturally enough gave rise to the doctrine of medicinal aggravations. Hahnemann at first gave a drop of the tincture at a dose, but he soon found that, in many cases at least, a much smaller quantity was sufficient to rouse the reactive energies of the diseased organism, and to effect the restoration of the patient's health. To divide a drop, Hahnemann resorted to the following process: With one drop of the tincture he mixed ninety-nine drops of alcohol, shook the mixture well in a corked vial, and thus obtained the first attenuation or potency of the original drug. To obtain the second attenuation, a drop of the first attenuation is mixed in a second vial with ninety-nine drops of alcohol, and shaken in a similar manner. The third attenuation is made from the second, and every succeeding attenuation from the preceding one. This process of attenuation has recently been continued, with a number of drugs, to the thousandth, two thousandth, and even the eight thousandth potency. This last potency constitutes a fractional portion of the original drop, the numerator of which being the drop, the denominator would form a line of cyphers which would probably stretch across one-third of the whole breadth of Manhattan island. The three hundreth potency is a fraction of a drop, the denominator of which contains no more nor less than six hundred cyphers; the eightieth potency is a fraction of a drop, the denominator of which contains one hundred and sixty cyphers; the denominator of the fortieth potency has eighty cyphers; that of the twentieth has forty cyphers; the twelfth has twenty-four; the sixth twelve; the third six cyphers. A vial full of the third attenuation, holding one hundred drops of medicine, contains, therefore, only the millionth part of a drop of the original tincture. It is with these so-called potencies that homœopathic physicians cure their patients. I may say here in passing, that the term "potency" is very badly understood by the uninitiated. It is commonly supposed that the power of the drug is developed in proportion as these attenuations of the original drop are multiplied. It is not in this sense that the term potentization or dynamization is understood by intelligent homœopathic physicians. By potency they understand the superior degree of curative adaptation to the disease which the original drug acquires by successive attenuations. This, at any rate, is my understanding of the term, although I am free to say that it was not thus understood either by Hahnemann or his disciples. The attenuated drug may, therefore, be actually weaker than the drug in its original or crude form, and yet it may possess more perfect, more precise curative relations to the disease, and, therefore, a superior faculty or power to remove it. Of course this removal is not effected by a revulsive action, but by a direct alteration of the disturbed nervous functions. But it will at once be perceived, that although a direct curative relation may exist between the attenuated drug and the disease, it would be absurd to infer from this fact the existence of an actual power, in a highly attenuated drug, to disturb the functions of the healthy organism. Are not the restoration of the disturbed functions to a state of health, and the disturbance of the healthy functions by medicinal agents, two opposites? How, then, could it be possible that the same rule should apply to both? If it require a highly attenuated drug to restore the functions from a state of disease to a state of health, how then could a similarly attenuated drug possess the power of altering the same functions from a state of health to one of disease? And yet, it is upon such paradoxes that a great many of our provings are based. Before retiring to bed in the evening, a few globules of the third, sixth, twelfth, thirtieth, sixtieth, or two hundredth attenuation are taken dry on the tongue; and if, next morning, the prover wakes up with a sick headache, or is troubled with the nightmare during the night, or perhaps with a little pinching and griping in the bowels, it is invariably the few globules that did all this mischief, whereas it is infinitely more probable that the globules were perfectly innocent of all this terrible work, and that the real cause of the trouble ought to have been traced perhaps to a cup of tea of an inferior quality, or a little stronger than usual, to the fatigue of the previous day, to a little excess at dinner, a bad cigar, a little exposure, and the like. One person among a thousand may be possessed of such a remarkable idiosyncratic sensitiveness to the action of particular drugs, that this action may yet be perceived even if the drug were highly attenuated; but would it be wise to suppose every body endowed with a similar idiosyncratic sympathy for the same drug, and to base upon such a hazardous theory a whole system of provings, which is to guide the physician in the important business of healing the sick, and perhaps in a case, too, where the patient's life is in imminent peril?

It is not merely the unreliability of the provings that renders a great number of our symptoms objectionable; it is the promiscuous and injudicious crowding, into the Materia Medica, of a great many pretended drugs which are not drugs properly speaking. One of the glaring errors of our modern symptom-hunters consists in the delusion, that every substance which is not positively required for the sustenance of the body, constitutes a drug, and is, therefore, endowed with medicinal properties. According to this doctrine, every animal which is not used for domestic purposes, from the smallest entozoon to the largest beast of prey; or every non-nutritious plant, from the most insignificant lichen to the tallest tree; or every mineral, from the minutest atom of dust floating on the sunbeam to the most ponderous boulder; in one word, every non-nutrient substance, of whatever form, color, or taste, is a drug, and, therefore, capable of curing certain forms of disease. This doctrine seems, on the face of it, so absurd, because so utterly incomplete and superficial, that it is a wonder to me why not one of the many enlightened thinkers in the homœopathic School should have raised his voice against it. The idea to prove the lion, the tiger, the hyena, the crocodile, the shark, the boa-constrictor, or to prescribe a few globules of the two or three thousandth potency of one of these ferocious beasts, seems certainly somewhat ludicrous; nor does the idea of proving an entozoon, though this animalcule may look ever so formidable when seen through the solar-microscope, inspire one with any more respect. Some things are made to be drugs; others fulfil purely chemical or technicological uses; others again exist to complete the great series of beings; others result from the temporary ignorance or neglect of man in properly taking care of his globe, draining the marshes and cultivating the soil; and some have undoubtedly been created in every kingdom of nature for therapeutic uses, and are, therefore, properly speaking, drugs. But there are few such substances as Arsenic, Belladonna, Aconite and the like, which are capable of altering the physiological functions of the organism in a positive, determinate, unchanging manner; whose relations to the organism can, therefore, be studied with scientific precision, and which can be made available for purposes of cure according to fixed and immutable laws. If the number of drugs were not limited; if their effects upon the organism were not fixed and certain; if their spheres of action in disease were not enclosed within unchangeable boundaries; if the ravings of certain homœopathic purists concerning modifications which they suppose are taking place in the action of drugs at certain intervals, had any foundation in truth; if Ipecacuanha, Aconite, Stramonium, or any other drug, did not affect the organism to-day, as they did when they were first created, medicine would be a contemptible agglomeration of foolish hypotheses and wild speculations, and would indeed appear to the reason that frightful chaos which the symptom-hunters of the homœopathic School bid fair to make it. To determine what is a drug, and what not, what is a drug-symptom and what merely an accidental disturbance of the functions, requires consummate judgment and unerring powers of observation. It seems contrary to common sense to offer as true and reliable indications of the curative action of drugs a series of vague, insignificant symptoms, which ninety-nine persons out of a hundred experience every day of their lives while attending to their daily pursuits, without having tasted or smelled a particle of medicine. Symptoms produced by the 12th, 18th, 30th, or even the 200th or 300th potency of a drug, forsooth! What rational and calm observer would be willing, in such a grave matter, to be guided by the ipse-dixit of men whose judgments are evidently blinded by the ridiculous mania of symptom-hunting? I have no doubt that the ten thousand trifling pains, sensations, pimples, spots, noises and the like, which they have recorded, were actually perceived; but, instead of being set down as evanescent and spontaneous phenomena of the hour, they were paraded before the profession as products of the drug, and incorporated in the Materia Medica as unimpeachable testimony in the solemn business of curing.

I am now prepared to devote a few moments to a critical examination of the law upon which the whole structure of homœopathy rests, I mean the celebrated formula, "*similia similibus*," or "like cures like." Its import has been abundantly explained. The series of symptoms which constitutes the natural disease, is effaced by applying to it a drug that is capable of producing a series of similar symptoms in the healthy organism. This similarity embraces, merely the outward form of the symptoms; it is a purely external similarity, totally distinct from the internal or essential condition of the organism. And yet, it is undeniable that disease is not merely a numerical juxtaposition of symptoms or subjective sensations, but a state of the organism, a disturbance of its normal laws. But a state of the organism has both quality and form. The sensually perceptible symptoms are the form, but not the quality of that state. Quality and form constitute an inseparable unit in the light of reason; they cannot be parted without appearing altered in their essential principles. Quality without form, is like love without wisdom, or like an idea without the word, or an attribute without a subject; and form without quality, is an unmeaning, lifeless, illogical, and deceptive appearance. What constitutes the real man? Is it not the outlines of his body, the shape of his nose, the color of his eyes or hair, the size of his head and mouth? All these external signs form a part of his identity, but they do not, by any means, make up the real man. It is, after all, the indwelling spirit, the man's passions and intellect, the purposes of his will and the energies and fire of his genius, that constitute the real man. A fact without its motive or quality, is not any thing, or it is a mere illusion. The character or value of the fact depends upon the purpose of the will from which it emanated. Murder is not murder, except in so far as there was a premeditated, positive design to take human life. Facts, disconnected from their internal motives, become unmeaning or deceptive appearances. In the great world, the seeming fact either saves or condemns a man. But in the light of reason, it is the purpose of the will that gives quality to the fact, and establishes its harmony with, or its opposition to, the laws of Divine justice and truth. Should not this same law prevail in medicine? Disease without symptoms, would be like the vital principle without a nervous system; but symptoms without internal conditions or relations, are unmeaning and valueless abstractions. According to Hahnemann's teaching, the strict homœopathist has no business to trouble himself about the internal state of the organism. If he is called to a patient who complains of sudden attacks of fainting and shortness of breath when walking about, anxiety, a bellows' noise in the region of the aorta, and a puffing of the hands, face, or the parts around the eyes; he would act contrary to the old-fashioned orthodox homœopathy, if he should take it into his head to inquire into the true meaning of these symptoms. A rational observer would be led to suspect the approach of hydrothorax, and if he should happen to know that the patient had a severe attack of inflammatory rheumatism years ago, he would moreover conclude that the abnormal sounds of the heart had some relation to the disease, and that its development probably depended upon, or, at any rate, co-existed with some organic affection of the heart which might baffle the best directed efforts of art. Supposing a patient complains of an aching pain in the kidney;

the pain shoots through the lower limb of the affected side, and is accompanied with a burning and throbbing sensation, sense of numbness and enlargement in the limb; at the same time there is a frequent urging to void the bladder, but the emission of urine which is dark and deposits a sediment at the bottom of the vessel, is rather difficult and painful; the bowels are costive, the complexion of the patient is rather sallow, at times a little flushed; pulse somewhat irritated; tongue coated whitish or brown; a good deal of thirst, but no appetite; flesh soft and flabby, and a tendency to general emaciation.

The strict Hahnemannian takes a record of these symptoms in their incoherent form, and then applies to his Materia Medica to find a medicine that produces a similar series of symptoms on the healthy. He will not find such a remedy in his whole Materia Medica; in such a case he takes the next best; it will disappoint him, but no matter; this is the regular mode of practising homœopathy; if the patient should die of his complaint, he dies by the book, and the infallibility of the treatment is not questioned for a moment. The physician who has trained his reason to look below the surface of the symptoms, and to understand their true meaning and internal connection and relation, would not be satisfied with a mere apparent similarity in prescribing for such a group of symptoms; he would want to understand the connection existing between that pain in the kidneys and the numbness, heat, and sense of enlargement in the extremity, together with the constitutional symptoms, the altered condition of the urinary secretions, the loss of appetite, the debility and emaciation, the heat and dryness of the skin; and he would arrive at the inevitable conclusion that some tuberculous disease is developing itself in the kidneys which, if at all curable, can only be controlled by the steady, well-sustained, and thoroughly understood application of specific means. The strict Hahnemannian gives his simile to-day, and if there be no change in the symptoms to-morrow, he selects some other drug, and then again another, and another, and another until he has fairly exhausted his whole Materia Medica. And yet the condition of the patient remains unaltered; the disorganization in the kidneys remains the same in its essential principles, and even if the symptoms should appear more or less modified to the sensual understanding, the tuberculous disease, whether better or worse, may nevertheless remain unchanged in all its inherent features, from the first appearance of the crude tubercle to the stage of purulent infiltration, and before the tribunal of true science, would require to be combated, not by a variety of medicines, but by means of specific remedies, applied with order, discrimination, and an enlightened conviction and knowledge of their curative powers.

Or, take a case of dysentery. The strict Hahnemannian views this disease as a mere derangement of symptoms, and treats it accordingly. If there be much fever he gives his Aconite; he would reject the Aconite as a dangerous intruder, if the fever should not be up to the boiling point, although the essential character of the disease and the constitutional condition of the patient might point to Aconite ever so much as the only true remedy in the case; if the discharges have a foul smell, he thinks of charcoal or Arsenic; if the patient feels cold, he tries to warm him up by a dose of Veratrum, and, if he should feel very weak, Arsenic or Cinchona is the proper tonic; an excessive tenesmus requires Mercurius or corrosive sublimate; if the stools have a greenish tinge, Chamomilla is prescribed; if there should be much pain in the bowels, Colocynth is applied to, and, if the blood begins to look foul or decomposed, Arsenic or charcoal again becomes the sheet-anchor. The symptom-doctor never thinks of studying the symptoms as an unitary group; he selects some prominent symptom, or a symptom that happens to strike his fancy, and then prescribes a remedy for this one symptom, in the expectation that its removal will cure the whole disease. But is it not evident that the pain in the bowels, the tenesmus, the discharge of blood, mucus and bile which is invariably present in dysentery, constitute one and the same alteration of the normal condition of the organism? Is it not wise to study these symptoms in their connection with the functions of the liver, and the general condition of the capillary system? This highest prerogative of the enlightened reason is rejected by the mere symptom-doctor as insane speculation and dangerous hypothesis; and yet it is this rational view of the physiological and pathological character of the symptoms that alone can lead us to the discovery, and determine the proper use of, the specific remedy in the case. A similar criticism applies to every other form of disease. Asiatic cholera for instance, presents a variety of symptoms, but what thinking practitioner will hesitate to view them as members of the same group, as effects of the same unvarying cause, as phenomena characterizing the same unitary disturbance of the physiological functions of the organism? Should not the remedy which is prescribed for this condition apply to the primary alteration of the nervous action, which, after all, determines the true character and meaning of all these apparently disconnected symptoms? Can there be an essential difference in an attack of cholera, between the cerebral congestion, the vomiting, the cramps, the rice-water discharges, the thirst, the burning in the epigastric region, the discoloration and shrivelling of the skin, the collapse of the pulse, the general sinking of strength and temperature? Is not this difference an illusion of the sensual understanding, or does it really exist in the light of the scientific reason?

The Hahnemannian homœopathist considers every symptom as a distinct morbid condition, not in theory, oh no! but in practice, constantly; and, agreeably to this method, he prescribes some thirty or forty different medicines for a disease which, if properly understood in its inmost or essential principles, is cured much more thoroughly, more expeditiously, and with infinitely more satisfaction to the physician and the patient by means of two or three specifically-adapted remedial agents. The symptomatic differences only appear such to the sensual understanding; the real difference resides in the structural organization of the parts over which the nerves and mucous membranes, these first recipients and reflectors of the morbid cause, are distributed. There is, so far as we know, no essential difference between the mucous membrane of the nose and that of the stomach; but, if either be irritated by the powdered root of Ipecacuanha, the irritation in the nose will be characterized by sneezing, and that of the stomach by vomiting or retching. This difference results from a difference in the structural organization of the parts, not from any essential difference in the action of the drug. It is the same with disease. Take the pneumogastric nerve, which is both a nerve of sensation and a nerve of motion. As a nerve of sensation it supplies the lining membrane of the respiratory and digestive passages, and it becomes a nerve of motion when it supplies the muscles and the muscular coats of the same canals. The pneumogastric nerve supplies branches, on the one hand, to the larynx, the lungs, and the heart; and, on the other, to the pharynx, the œsophagus, the stomach and the solar plexus. These various parts could not fulfil their organic functions, without their inherent vitality being constantly stimulated by the nerve. The nerve is essentially the same in all its branches; the functional differences reside in the structural organization of the parts over which the branches are distributed.

These facts being well established by physiological and anatomical researches, let us inquire into the practical results to which they necessarily lead. Suppose we have to deal with a diseased condition, an acute irritation of the pneumo-gastric nerve in all its parts, by what symptoms would such an irritation be characterized? They would appear exceedingly diversified and might even seem disconnected; but the scientific reason would easily connect them into an unitary group, and would trace the symptomatic differences to their appropriate source, namely to the differences in the structural organization of the parts affected. In the larynx we might have dryness, soreness, heat, titillation, a constant desire to cough and hawk; in the chest we might note a soreness, a stricture and oppression across the part, or even asthmatic paroxysms; the affection in the epigastric region might be characterized by sensitiveness, fulness and distention, a burning or throbbing distress, an aching pain, or a sensation as if a cold stone were obstructing the parts; beside all these symptoms we might have acidity of the stomach, spitting up of the food after eating, palpitation of the heart, soreness of the bowels, looseness or constipation, not to mention a variety of other symptoms, all of which might seem disconnected to the unreasoning observer, but which the rational physician would not fail to set down as an unitary irritation of the pneumo-gastric nerve; essentially the same in the whole tract of the nerve, and, therefore, requiring the same consistent treatment, whatever that might be.

In the critical remarks which I have offered, it has been my endeavor to show,

First, that the literal interpretation of the homœopathic formula "*similia similibus curantur*," does not admit of a comprehensive and strictly scientific application in the treatment of disease;

Secondly, that a vast number of the symptoms by which homœopathic physicians profess to be guided in the selection of their remedies for particular cases of disease, is not only unreliable, but positively false and imaginary;

Thirdly, that the practice which some physicians have adopted, of crowding indiscriminately into the Materia Medica any substance which happens to strike their fancy, or to harmonize with their theoretical illusions, is condemnable, because it has a tendency to convert the Materia Medica into a huge curiosity-shop filled with insignificant and worthless trifles; and

Fourthly, that the law "*similia similibus*" refers purely to an outward similarity between the symptoms of the disease and those of the drug, but that it takes no cognizance of the essential states of the organism, and that, without a lucid appreciation of these states by the scientific reason, their phenomenal indications, the symptoms, remain unmeaning, incoherent and deceptive abstractions.

Now, if all this criticism be true, and it strikes me that I have not merely asserted any thing, but that I have substantiated my objections to the orthodox practice of homœopathy by fair argument, it is proper to inquire: If there be a fundamental principle upon which the true science of medicine rests, what is the principle that will secure a positive, certain, unerring, and expeditious treatment in every case of disease? This is a question of vast import, and its satisfactory solution demands perhaps more knowledge than I can bring to bear upon it. Nevertheless, I will enter upon the task of showing the existence and elucidating the formula of a true therapeutic law, and beg the reader to peruse the third part of this work with a desire of doing justice to the doctrines therein advanced.

PART III.

FORMULA

OF THE

HOMŒOPATHIC LAW,

AS SUGGESTED BY THE

Union of Pharmacodynamics and Therapeutics,

UPON A

PHYSIOLOGICO-PATHOLOGICAL BASIS.

PART III.

Medicine must either have come to man by revelation or by the slow process of observation. It is not probable that Providence ever revealed to man the uses of drugs by any other method than that of experience. If he did possess such a revelation at any time, it is certain that all traces of it have disappeared, and that, as far as existing records bear us testimony, medicine is emphatically a science, which, under the over-ruling Providence of God, has been developed by human reason, and is enlarged and perfected more and more, by a more accurate perception, and a more universal unfolding of the facts that constitute its legitimate domain. We can easily imagine that, at one period, in the first ages of the world, man must have been totally ignorant of all distinction between poisons and nutrient substances, and that, not being posessed of instinct which, to the animal, is a perfectly safe guide in the selection of its food, he may have mistaken the deleterious berry of Belladonna for some pleasant fruit, or a poisonous mushroom for an innocuous vegetable. The probability is that man frequently allowed himself to be deceived by appearances, and that he was frequently beguiled into the notion that, what seemed beautiful and attractive to the eye, must be pleasant and useful as an article of diet. Reason tells us that experience and observation were man's first guides towards the acquisition of knowledge, and that his first initiation into the properties of poisons, must have been the fruit of painful and fatal mistakes. But a knowledge of the properties of poisons did not by any means imply a knowledge of their uses as medicinal agents. This knowledge is a perception of the reason, and, though based upon and confirmed by experience, yet it is not primarily suggested by, or derived from it. It is not probable that sickness existed before a knowledge of drugs was acquired by man; this would have been contrary to the order of Providence.

Man probably had learned by experience, that Ipecacuanha and Lobelia caused vomiting, and that Jalap purged the bowels long before a case of disease occurred. And when disease finally invaded the world, the probability is that a good many persons had to be sick, before the idea that a curative relation existed between poisons and diseases, dawned upon man's infantile reason; and when, finally, a first perception of the uses of drugs developed itself in the human mind, by what other principle could man have been guided in their application than a principle of antagonism? He knew that when he felt cold, he could neutralize the cold by warming himself; or that, when he felt hungry or thirsty, hunger and thirst would disappear after eating or drinking. Was it not natural that this daily experience should have been applied to the use of drugs in disease, and that, if the bowels, for instance, were constipated, man should have selected for the removal of that constipation some drug which he knew produced the opposite effect? Indeed, this became the general principle of cure so far as it was applicable. Medicines were prescribed that had a tendency to produce effects contrary to those of the disease. This principle, which has been perpetuated under the well known formula of "*contraria contrariis curantur*," is however, liable to serious objections. One of the principal objections is, that it is impossible to find a contrarium to disease. What is the contrarium of a sick-headache? Of colic? Of pneumonia? Of paralysis? Of pleurisy? or of almost any other disease you may name? Diseases have no contraries, and the principle "*contraria contrariis*," is therefore, at most, a theoretical sophism. But even in cases where the principle might have been applied with a show of reason, for instance, in a case of diarrhœa or constipation, it was soon discovered that the use of a contrary medicine frequently had the effect of aggravating the condition of the patient, and rendering his complaint more obstinate in the end. It was seen that the principle "*contraria contrariis*" is a perfect rule, when a palliating effect is to be obtained; that it applies perfectly to the common processes of life; that hunger is satisfied by food, thirst quenched by drinks, cold is removed by heat, and heat tempered by cold; and that, by all these palliative gratifications, the organism is strengthened, and the harmony of its functions preserved. But it was likewise perceived, that when this principle of contraries was elevated to the rank of a curative law, it became a dangerous fallacy. As man became better acquainted with the operations of the nervous system, he sought to bring the treatment of disease more in harmony with the eternal principles of nature. It was observed that an internal pain would sometimes cease with the appearance of an eruption or boil upon the skin, or that some lingering disease, a weakness of the stomach, an oppression on the chest, a headache, a lingering fever, debility, and so forth, would disappear spontaneously with the breaking out of a sore, or of some eruption upon the chest, head, or extremities. These observations gave rise to the so-called derivative or revulsive method of treatment. This method, too, as well as the palliative method, is a legitimate mode of affording relief to the patient, as long as it is not carried beyond its true boundaries of palliation; there cannot be any reasonable objection to a warm poultice, a mustard-plaster, a pitch-plaster, as long as the sufferings of the patient are really palliated by such applications; but when the principle of counter-irritation is made the basis of a compact system of treatment, it then leads to results which are justly condemned by every friend of man as frightful aberrations of an insane and barbarous science. Will it be believed by an enlightened and refined posterity, that the great and sacred purpose of the healing art, which is to alleviate, and not to inflict suffering, was ever sought to be attained by scorching a man's back with a red-hot iron, or burning his skin by a slow fire? And yet, these practices which have been repudiated now-a-days by every true-hearted physician, were once the fashionable tortures which the cruel genius of man had devised for the relief of the sick.

Various theories were imagined by the leaders of medical science to account not only for the phenomena of disease, but also to construct the edifice of medicine upon a scientific basis. It is well known that, among these various classes of medical philosophers, the humoralists and the vitalists hold the principal rank. The humoralists explain disease upon the principle of vitiated humors in the body, and their whole treatment is directed towards correcting or expelling the humors. The vitalists attribute the phenomena of disease to a deranged action of the vital forces, but, although they differ from the humoralists in their theory of disease, their practice is pretty much the same, and whatever differences may exist, principally result from differences of taste and judgment in the individual practitioners. Drugs were made to harmonise with preconceived theories; if different classifications of the Materia Medica were adopted by the authors of new medical systems, it was not because the essential properties of drugs were better known, but because the classifications previously in use, did not suit the new definitions. The great question, to study the therapeutic properties of drugs without reference to any preconceived medical theory, remained yet to be solved. Evidently a true science of pharmacodynamics should inform us of the precise effects of Laudanum, of Arsenic, of Belladonna, or of any other drug upon the human organism. How is this knowledge to be acquired? By speculative theories, by accidental observations, or by systematic provings upon the healthy organism? There was a time when speculative theories constituted the chief means of determining the therapeutic uses of drugs. These theories were based upon the grossest sensual perceptions. It was the shape, taste, or color of a drug that indicated its relation to disease. Such gross fantasies no longer misguide the reason; and the authors of our modern treatises of pharmacodynamics are not satisfied with any thing short of actual observation in determining the uses of drugs and assigning them a proper place in their classifications. Accidental poisonings are not sufficient for a complete and correct investigation of the properties of drugs, were it for no other reason than because all the more delicate effects of the poison upon the nervous system remain unheeded under the fright and the excitement consequent upon the discovery of the dangerous mistake; and, if the poisoning should be a voluntary act, the self-destroyer will certainly not amuse himself with watching the gradual evolution of symptoms, while his whole soul is bent on death as the ultimate result of his insane proceeding. Nevertheless, a great many, and probably the most valuable contributions to our Materia Medica, have been obtained from cases of poisoning. For, an observing physician was frequently called in time to note all the more striking effects of the poison while listening to a report of the case and preparing his antidote. And some of these cases occurred so frequently, that a tolerably accurate picture of the physiological effects of many poisons was gradually obtained in a long series of successive observations. Still the sketch was incomplete, the broad outlines were drawn, but all the more delicate shades which alone could give tone and character to the picture, were wanting. These delicate, but truly characteristic effects of the poison would probably never be revealed to a casual observer. They had to be studied, and, for this purpose, the poison had to be introduced into the organism according to a definite method, in measured quantities, at regular intervals, and while the prover enjoyed perfect bodily and mental health. More than one eminent physiologist had pointed out the necessity of this mode of experimentation; but it was reserved for the genius and perseverance of the founder of homœopathy to pave the way for a positive science of pharmacodynamics, by instituting a series of drug-provings, which, for reliability, comprehensiveness, accuracy of observation and devotion to science, will commend themselves at all times to the confidence and admiration of every friend of scientific truth.

Let us now suppose every drug to be known; every effect of the drug carefully and correctly ascertained and universally acknowledged: it is evident that this solves only the first half of the problem, and that the other half, the application of drugs to the treatment of disease, or, in other words, the conversion of drugs into remedial agents, remains yet to be disposed of. Supposing we are fully and positively acquainted with the physiological effects of all drugs, does this knowledge reveal to us their therapeutic uses? Does it tell us, for instance, in what way the effects of Mercury are related to disease? Or to what diseases? These are now the important points that require our earnest and unprejudiced attention.

The first notions of the therapeutic uses of certain substances in nature were based upon purely sensual perceptions. A certain substance was known to purge the bowels, and, when the bowels were constipated, this substance was resorted to to move them. This was a material mode of proceeding; material results were sought to be removed by material causes. The natural condition of the bowels, viz: their confined state, was looked upon as the real disease, and the removal of their contents by means of a cathartic was supposed to constitute a cure. This was a sensual system of medicine, based upon phenomenal appearances, but without any rational conception of the inmost or real nature of disease, and therefore deprived of a true law of cure. For, the rational observer has no difficulty in perceiving that the confined state of the bowels is merely a material indication of an altered condition of the normal vital action, and that, unless this abnormal alteration is exactly met by a corresponding curative influence, the bowels may be temporarily or palliatively forced into action, without the vital economy of the organism being at all relieved of its embarrassment. Disease is not a mere assemblage of sensual phenomena, but a state of the organism, no more than man is a mere delineation of outward features, but a living form of thoughts and affections. It is to this state of the organism that the remedial agent must respond; otherwise a cure by therapeutic means is impossible. Disease is the problem, as it were, and the remedial agent its solution. Or disease and its true remedy may be said to be the terminal points of a straight line. As there can be but one true answer to a question, or one true solution to a problem, so there can be but one true remedy to a disease. To be sure, a disease may consist of a variety of states, which may develope themselves in a regular series, and each state may require a different remedy; but whatever state prevails at any one time, must be met by its appropriate remedy; it cannot be acted upon by any other remedy than the one which is specifically related to it as a curative agent, and corresponds to all its essential characteristics. What other conclusion could the rational mind arrive at, in viewing a list of the drugs and their complete effects upon the organism? If we know that it is the business of these drugs to cure disease, will not the question force itself upon our minds: Will any of these drugs cure any disease? Or will some particular drug cure some particular disease? The idea that any drug will cure any disease, is so manifestly absurd that reason adopts with delight the other alternative, that a particular disease has to be cured by some particular drug. The question then is: what drug will cure a given disease, and by what indications is this drug to be recognized? The answer to this question belongs to the domain of reason; pure experimentation and the observation of natural phenomena constitute the legitimate sphere of the sensual understanding; but reason determines the law which disposes the facts into an orderly system, and unites them into a general truth. Here is the great error which Hahnemann committed in laying down his law "*similia similibus curantur.*" This law is simply a perception of the sensual understanding, not a conception of the reason. Remove the sensually "perceptible phenomena of disease by applying to them analogous sensually-perceptible drug-symptoms; this is the rule in strict Hahnemannian practice, and this rule is just as much a sensual perception as the old-fashioned rule of removing sensually-perceptible symptoms of disease by means of sensually-perceptible contrary drug-symptoms. There is this difference between the two formulas of "*similia similibus,*" and "*contraria contrariis,*" that the idea of contraries in medicine is a fallacy both in practice and theory; the idea of similars is a fallacy only in practice, although even there partially true; but, in theory, it is a truth, but only an *apparent* truth; it is not *the* truth, as has been abundantly shown in the second part of this work. A vague similarity between the natural effects of Quinine and the symptoms of fever and ague, is said to have led Hahnemann to the idea that a similarity of this kind between the symptoms of disease and the artificial drug-symptoms, must exist in every case where the drug is to become a true remedial agent; and he thereupon instituted his provings in order to construct a Materia Medica in harmony with his preconceived theory. Although the followers of Hahnemann claim this mode of proceeding as resulting from a strict application of the Baconian philosophy of induction to the principles and practice of medicine, yet it must strike every unprejudiced observer, that Hahnemann conducted his argument wrong side foremost, and that a strictly inductive process of reasoning would have required him, first to obtain a complete and accurate knowledge of the natural effects of drugs upon the healthy organism, and then, by a process of pure reasoning, to determine the law of cure which the natural action of drugs and the essential characteristics of disease seemed to indicate as the true basis of the healing art. What Hahnemann has failed to accomplish, let us now try to accomplish for him.

Hahnemann's Materia Medica Pura is a model of exact and patient observations of the effects of drugs upon the healty organism; but the thousands of symptoms of which this Materia Medica is composed, are not connected by any logical or internal bond; they constitute an incoherent list of pains, nervous sensations, eruptions, dreams, abnormal mental conditions, which do not reflect the image of a single disease, in a clear, unmistakeable and complete manner. But, is not the highest object which we seek to attain in all drug-provings, to know what diseases the drugs will cure safely, thoroughly, and expeditiously? A mere abstract knowledge of the natural effects of drugs, would be hardly worth the trouble of inflicting systematic pains and privations upon the organism in a regular course of drug-provings. And yet, a mere abstract knowledge of isolated, incoherent drug-symptoms, is all that the present Materia Medica conveys to the student of homœopathy. To make it practicable, the arrangement of its symptoms has been subjected to various modifications. In its present form, the Materia Medica is in harmony with the fundamental law of the Hahnemannian practice of homœopathy, and is, therefore, liable to the same objections as the law itself. It does not exhibit the curative relation of a single drug to any known disease, in a positive and unmistakeable manner. Let a physician study the homœopathic Materia Medica, from beginning to end, with conscientious care, and with a willing, open, and capable mind, and let him then, with his brain stocked with symptoms, step to the bed-side of a patient, and undertake to prescribe for a case of pneumonia, of inflammation of the brain, liver, pleura, or for any other inflammatory, nervous, or cutaneous disease: his Materia Medica will sadly disappoint him in the hour of need, and, bewildered and spurred on by the sting of necessity, of confounded ambition and the desire to help his patient, he will be reduced to the inevitable dilemma of either sacrificing his patient, or else resorting to a convenient routine-practice, and confessing, in his inmost conscience, to the inadequacy of the means he had so implicitly and generously relied upon. This is what most homœopathic physicians are doing. The existing practice of homœopathy is a species of empirical routine, nothing else. Every disease is treated with a certain set of remedies, with perhaps slight differences in the order of succession, or the size of the doses, but it is Aconite for fever, Belladonna and Mercurius for sore throat, Aconite and Phosphorus for pneumonia, Colocynth for colic; or it is Arsenic for burning pains, Nux vomica for dragging or bearing-down pains, Bryonia for flashing or shooting pains, Cocculus for spasmodic menstrual pains; or, once in a while, a repertory, the contents of which are arranged according to a certain order, may be consulted for some out-of-the-way symptom; but, as a general rule, the practice of the homœopathic school has become a routine-practice, which undoubtedly, had its first origin in the provings of the Materia Medica, but which has derived its development from the genius and tact of individual practitioners, and its sanction and consummation from a more or less satisfactory and brilliant experience. And what else could the practice of homœopathy be with a Materia Medica where the symptoms of all diseases are mixed up in one confused mass; where scientific order is superseded by an illogical, repulsive, soul-withering uniformity in the exterior arrangement of the symptoms;

where all physiological relations of the symptoms, are either completely effaced or left unexplained, and where cunning devices have to be resorted to in the place of eternal principles, for the purpose of introducing some kind of order into this dreary and uninteresting chaos of details, and making it available in practice? The mere symptom-doctor is obliged to visit his patients with his repertory or clinical guide in the pocket of his overcoat, and, after he has examined the symptoms, not the patient or his disease, to depend upon his book for an indication of the medicine, to the effects of which the symptoms of the disease seem to resemble, and which is, therefore, supposed to be the true remedial agent in this case. But is it not humiliating for a physician to be reduced to the necessity of carrying his dead books from door to door, instead of consulting the living reason, and deriving from its wisdom a true knowledge of both the disease and the remedy? Pharmacodynamics has no value except as the handmaid of therapeutics, and in every rational Materia Medica, the action of drugs should be explained with reference to the diseases to which the drugs are specifically related as curative agents. Let me now proceed to an examination of the bond that unites pharmacodynamics or the science of the medicinal properties of drugs and therapeutics, or the science of applying them to the purposes of the healing art, into one harmonious unit.

If we had a perfect knowledge of the real nature of disease, and of the inmost principle of our drugs, a therapeutic law would become a thing of mathematical precision; but, in the absence of this knowledge we have to content ourselves with an approximation to the truth, and to depend, in a great measure, upon the pure reason for a definition of disease and upon its true relation to remedial agents.

Disease is not, as is generally supposed, a state of the system opposite to health. This may seem paradoxical; and, nevertheless, if disease, generally speaking, were the opposite of health, this general truth must certainly remain true in its particular applications. There must, therefore, be a quality or state of health opposite to typhus-fever, another quality of health opposite to measles, another to rheumatism, another to paralysis, another to small-pox, another to dropsy, or, in one word, every form of disease must have an opposite state or quality of health. This is, evidently, not the case; hence we infer that the general principle, being false in all its particular applications, must, itself, be a fallacy, an illusion of the sensual understanding. Now then, if health and disease are neither opposite, nor identical states of existence, they must hold towards each other relations of more or less; health, therefore, is a less degree of disease than what we generally term disease; and disease is a less degree of health than what we generally term health. In adopting this mode of reasoning I use the terms health and disease in an absolute sense, meaning by health the perfect harmony, and by disease the perfect disharmony of the physiological functions of the organism. A man's health may be so nearly perfect that usage has justified the expression: He enjoys perfect health; but as long as human society and this planet remain invaded by disease, we cannot, strictly speaking, say that perfect health exists in a single instance; there is more or less of it in a given case, but it is never perfect. Taking the perfect equilibrium of the functions as our standard of comparison, we may say that disease is an inferior or lesser degree of health or health disturbed; so that, even in disease, the idea of health is still preserved: without health, disease would not be any thing; whatever it is, it is with reference to health. Even in disease, the orderly arrangement of the organism still exists; the play of the physiological functions, although impaired and embarrassed by hostile influences, is still the same in its essential principles, and we have to depend upon these very functions for the successful operation of our drugs in their efforts to restore the disturbed equilibrium of the system. Disease, therefore, cannot mean a derangement of the inmost vital harmony; for, in such a case, all our attempts at restoring it, would be useless, and death would inevitably result in every case. More than this, if the life-principle which pervades the inmost organism as an immaterial agent, and is identical with the life-principle of the Creator, from whom it originally emanated, and by whom it is unceasingly strengthened and developed, could be at all tainted by disease, the Divine Being himself would be exposed to its disturbing agency and the universal order would be annihilated. The material organism may perish, but man's essential life can never be destroyed; on the contrary, death must simply be the evolution of a more beautiful, more harmonious, more heavenly life, the birth of the soul's true organism that shall live and grow for ever as a form of love and wisdom. This organism can never be invaded by disease; it is only its material counterpart, the earthly body, whose functions are subject to alterations and whose organs decay. Wherever the inmost or essential life-principle exists in all its fulness and strength, disease can never penetrate. In order not to be misunderstood, let me state very fully and explicitly that it is an immaterial, spiritual life-principle that I allude to, in contra-distinction to the material vital principle which is possessed even by the brute creation. The supposition of the existence of a soul in man does not sufficiently account for the phenomena of life unless we admit the existence of an intermediate spiritual organism, which is the soul's essential embodiment and mediately supports and feeds every fibre of the living frame. Without the renovating aid of this spiritual organism, which is unassailable by disease, the material body, if once deranged, could never recover its harmony; it would inevitably perish. If the soul were not universally and minutely connected with every least portion, nerve or fibre, of the material organism by means of an exactly similar spiritual organism, how could the soul be of the least use to the support and renovation of the material frame? I am fully aware that, in the opinion of many physiologists and metaphysicians, the soul is merely a thinking and feeling abstraction, a vaporous, shapeless and undefinable something; but these philosophers establish the same relation between the soul and body that deists fancy exists between God and his universe. He is merely a selfish, unfeeling looker-on; he has made his universe a self-existing machine, and man has been endowed by him with reason for the purpose of regulating his own affairs and the affairs of his globe in such a manner that he shall either derive pleasure or misery from the administration of his office. But this doctrine of God is suggested by the mere appearances of things. The sensual philosopher cannot imagine that a world where the divine principles of justice and charity constitute the exception, and heartless self-love, cunning, tyranny and hatred, the ruling principles of order, can be, in the remotest degree, cared for by Providence; and yet, with a little reason, he might know that God can never separate himself from his creation, and that it can only be, and remain, what it is, in so far as God is, and remains, in it. God cannot divide himself, and yet, he must either do this, or else Creation would relapse into its original chaos or nothing; for, if the Divine Principle should withdraw itself from Creation, what would support this mechanism? The in-dwelling power? But that power is a part of God, essentially and eternally one with him, with his love and his wisdom. God's Providence, therefore, pervades every nook and corner of the universe, watches over every trembling leaf, decks the budding flower with its hue of beauty, feeds the warbling lark, and leads man, step by step, towards a higher life of love and truth. And what God, and his eternally-true, his ever-present, ever-watchful, self-existing, all-providing love and wisdom are to the universe generally, that the soul and its spiritual organism are to the human body in particular. It is from this spiritual organism that the body exists; the spiritual organism preserves it not like a *deus ex machina*, but by virtue of an intimate, fixed and perfect union which, in fact, makes man a living man, a feeling, thinking, and acting being.

The spiritual organism, personating God's Providence to the material frame, is forever free from all disease. This organism is not an aggregate of metaphysical abstractions, but an organization embodying the soul's essential life, its active powers termed passions, affections, emotions, impulses, and the inherent forms thereof which are the spontaneous or voluntary thoughts of the mind. These constituent principles are substances, of a transcendently ethereal nature, if you please, but infinitely more real than the material frame and its inherent vital principle. For, these ethereal substances are imperishable, whereas the material organism is destined to decay. The spiritual organism is governed by its own sovereign laws of orderly freedom, and is the supreme, though scarcely known regulator, of man's sensual life, which it endeavors to expand into such directions and forms as agree with the soul's essential conscience, which is but too often in direct antagonism to the acquired conscience of the actual man and to all his modes of life and habits of belief. The material body cannot enjoy perfect health until it has become absolutely subordinate to the influences of the spiritual organism, and moves, acts, feels, tastes, in one word, lives in all respects agreeably to the dictates of the soul's essential wisdom and genuine impulses and affections. The union between the spiritual and material organisms may not be sufficiently perfect to preserve the latter in health. We must not forget that no perfect adjustment between man's spiritual and material natures has yet been attained, and that the inmost principle of life in man, of which it is stated in the sacred record that God blew into man's nostrils the breath of lives, is anxious and willing to unite itself with the material organism in perfect freedom, but that it cannot force its law of order upon this organism. Before a perfect union between the internal spiritual and the external material organism can exist, reason, which is the soul's wisdom, has, in the first place, to reveal to man's sensual understanding the true order of his physical life: the production, preparation and use of food; the various industrial pursuits, architecture, education, social government, and the whole complex of our social rules, customs and institutions, have to be known and organized agreeably to the eternal and unchanging principles of Divine Truth and Justice, before the internal spiritual organism, the soul's true life, can infuse its regenerating energies into the material frame, and transform it again into what God had originally made it, a perfect tabernacle of divine harmony and beauty. The disunion between the internal spiritual and the external material organisms must be characterized by sensations of pain, as the perfect union between these two organisms would be characterized by sensations of pleasure. Otherwise by what signs should man recognize the disunion? This disunion may embrace the whole of man's interests, his affections, ideas, tastes, talents and bodily powers. It is the peculiar province of the physician to look at this disunion as existing between the bodily life as it is, and as it ought to be agreeably to the demands and indications of the internal reason. In a general sense this disunion may be marked by an absence of the blissful feeling of buoyant health; and, in a special sense, the disunion may be characterized by positive sensations of pain and by abnormal appearances which indicate the presence of, but are not, the disease. Disease is a condition, a state of the material organism; it is a sign of its deviation from the essential order of the soul's divinely-inspired love and wisdom, agreeably to whose indications and demands the material man should regulate his outward existence. For present purposes of cure a knowledge of the real nature of disease is not material. Some view it as the invasion of the material organism by some evil spirit; others define it as an abnormal condition of the vital forces; others again attribute it to the presence of vitiated humors, forgetting that these vitiated humors themselves might very properly be looked upon as the disease. I have defined disease as a state of disunion of the external material organism from the essential or eternally-true life of the internal spiritual man. Generally this disunion will exist until man shall have realized a perfect life of truth in all things, in religion, science, art, industry, education and social government. Specially this disunion may become more particularly manifest in extraordinary cases of deviation from the laws of order, such as exposure to the sun's scorching rays, to draughts of air, blasting winds and deleterious miasms; or abuse of food or drink, hard work, starvation, undue fatigue of any kind, and a variety of other circumstances which develope a train of fixed, and constantly-recurring phenomena, pains, eruptions, nervous derangements and the like, that constitute the common diseases of man. Hahnemann and some of his followers, carried away by an insane opposition to pathology, even to its truths, have sought to destroy all classification of diseases, and to supplant it, except in the case of miasmatic diseases, by a purely numerical arrangement of the symptoms without order or physiological connection. But to the judicious observer the phenomena of disease appear as definite and logical as the phenomena of health; physiological functions serve as a basis to pathological states and symptoms; the true physician invariably connects dyspepsia with the healthy process of digestion, or explains fever with reference to the normal state of the circulation. It is proper and necessary to first account for the physiology of a sick headache before we can undertake to cure it, just as necessary as it is for a surgeon to understand the relation of the artery to the accompanying vein and nerve before he can proceed to apply his ligature.

But a knowledge of the physiology of disease does not explain its essence, any more than a knowledge of the physiological functions accounts for the inmost principle of life. Evidently a cooling draught of air is no essential cause of disease; if it were, it would disturb the physiological functions, more or less, in every case, nor would it generally be accompanied with a sensation of pleasantness; but it is well known that thousands can sit, or even sleep, in a draught without hurting themselves; thousands will bear exposure to wind, rain, poisonous miasms with impunity; how then could these conditions themselves be the primary causes of disease? If they were, they would produce, in every case, more or less uniform and positive disturbances of the organism, and a cure would invariably follow the removal of these causes, upon the well known principle, "*cessante causa, cessat effectus*," when the cause ceases, the effect ceases likewise. But it is well known that a considerable period sometimes has to elapse after the cessation of the exposure, before the real disease develops itself in the organism. It is true, there is a period of incubation in other diseases, during which there is no apparent disturbance of the organism; and yet, the disease is developing itself all the time, like the germ under ground, and, after a while, it breaks forth with all its symptomatic characteristics. The principle of disease is, therefore, present in the organism from the first invasion to the ultimate termination of the malady. But this observation cannot apply to the former series of apparent causes. The same cause, if acting under the same circumstances, must produce the same effect; but the same exposure will occasion, in one, an inflammation of the lungs; in another, a mere cold in the head; in a third, dysentery; in a fourth, typhus; in a fifth, ophthalmia; in a sixth, inflammatory rheumatism. From this diversity of effects we may safely infer, that they have to be traced to more specific causes than the apparent exposure, and that this exposure can at most, only be regarded as a means of enabling the real cause to act.

According to the vitalists, disease is a purely dynamic alteration of the vital forces, and they have expended a tremendous quantity of acute logic to prove the truth of this fallacy. But, if disease were simply a dynamic disturbance of the functional harmony of the organism, it would necessarily follow that the vital principle, which, in its inmost essence, constitutes one of the infinite forms of the divine love and wisdom, can, at one and the same time, be a state of goodness and evil, of order and confusion, of harmony and discord, which is manifestly impossible and absurd. Nor can vitiated humors be the primary cause of disease in the organism, for the humors are results of the vital action, and it is not so much the vitiated humors, as their vitiation, that constitutes the real disease. Now, if disease be not directly caused by the circumambient influences of atmosphere, climate, food; or if it be not merely an abnormal condition of the vital essence, or consist of vitiated humors, what else then can it be, but a thing of its own, a vital spirit, an ethereal principle or miasm, or any thing else you please, but, at all events, a substantial something, obeying its own order of existence, which it endeavors to impose upon the organism, and which the organism tries to resist? This struggle between the organism and the principle of disease, is characterized by pains and by various abnormal sensations and appearances, by which it manifests itself to the sensual understanding. The understanding perceives, and the reason determines the character of, these phenomena, and their relation to each other, and to the organism and its particular parts. To the understanding, therefore, the disease seems an assemblage of symptomatic appearances, pains, nervous derangements; but the reason views it as an internal state of the organism resulting from the invasion of an hostile principle, and its struggle with the organic vital forces. What this morbific principle is in its inmost essence, is just as difficult to determine, in the present state of our knowledge, as the inmost nature of the vital principle itself. Nevertheless, we may offer suggestions which, although more or less hypothetical, may be in harmony with universally admitted facts. And, in the first place, it is evident, that, at whatsoever infinite a distance the vital principle may exist from man in its primary source, yet with its emanations, it must surround and pervade the organism, even to its inmost parts, just as the emanations of the material sun pervade the tissue or grain of every known substance of material nature. The fact that the vital principle has never yet been discovered in the crucible of the chemist, is no reason why its presence in and around man should be denied.

There was a time when the atmospheric air was supposed to be an elementary body, and yet, we know now that it is composed of a number of other elements, among which oxygen and nitrogen bear a conspicuous part. A vital sphere may, and I should say, must constitute the inmost nature of the surrounding medium; for, the universe having once been called into existence as a complete and compact unit, God has confided its preservation and progressive development to mediate forces which act in a continuous series from the spiritual-ethereal down to the sensual-material order, and finally, by acting upon and embodying themselves in the molecules of matter, give rise to the infinitely-varied substances of nature, distinguished from each other by their shape, color, taste, weight, chemical and physical attributes, and more essentially by the uses which man is enabled to accomplish by means of them. It is upon these uses that their value to man depends. These uses are as varied as the things themselves; every thing fulfils uses, even those things which we call hurtful. But it is evident that there must be an essential difference between a thing which serves to develope, strengthen, and beautify the organism; and a thing which, by its direct action upon the organism, tends to disturb and destroy it. This antagonism must depend upon essential differences in the inmost principles, the spiritual-ethereal forces, or whatever they may be, which were mediately instrumental in creating either the useful articles of food or the deleterious poisons. For, the chemical constituents of cauliflower and stramonium are the same, except that they exist in different proportions. But that which makes them to exist in different proportions, this inherent principle, without whose permanent presence in the inmost tissues the things would cease to be what they are, and return again into their original molecular state; this principle differs in different substances, and is either good or evil in its relations with the organism in a state of harmony. But, if it be true that God looked at every thing after he had created it, and said it was good, then how could any created substance affect the organism as something absolutely evil? Every thing must be *useful* to the organism in some way, and the use of a thing must depend upon the state in which the organism happens to be. If, then, a thing be hurtful to the organism in health, it must be useful to it when diseased. Reason tells us that the highest use which a poison can fulfil in the human organism, is to restore the diseased organism to health. A poison which is capable of fulfilling such uses, is essentially a remedial agent, or, generally speaking, a drug; and, inasmuch as each drug is specifically different from every other, it follows that each has specific therapeutic uses to fulfil towards the organism in a state of disease. In other words, the diseased organism holds specific relations to a particular drug, and the purpose and ultimate result of these relations, if realized in action, must be the restoration of the organism to health, in the most direct, safe, agreeable, and expeditious manner. This curative relation must be based upon some essential sympathy existing between the drug and the disease, not between the drug and the organism; for we have seen that the essential relation between the drug and the organism is one of antagonism, not of sympathy; whatever sympathy there is, must therefore exist between the drug and the disease, and as a matter of course, the more intimate this sympathy, the more certain and positive becomes the curative relation; so that, if the sympathy be perfect, the curative relation becomes perfect. This perfect sympathy between the drug and the disease can only exist on one condition, which is, that the principle of disease and the inmost or mediately-curative principle of the drug should be essentially the same, in fact identical. The same morbific force, which, by invading the organism under appropriate circumstances, developes a certain series of pains and derangements which we term disease: by acting upon the material molecules of nature, embodies itself in the shape of some poisonous animal, plant, or mineral, which, in its turn, by its action upon the healthy organism, would be capable of reproducing the symptoms which the original morbific principle had developed. Hence, what more natural method of finding out what drug holds specific curative relations to a particular disease, than to introduce this drug into a sufficient number of healthy organisms, according to some definite method, in determinate quantities and at regular intervals, for the purpose of developing the whole series of its natural effects upon man? But in order that we may be enabled to determine the specific curative relation of a certain drug to some particular disease, it is not necessary that the series of drug-symptoms should correspond exactly with the series of the natural morbid symptoms in all its details.

The object of proving is not to elicit this perfect correspondence between the symptoms. The object of every rational proving is, to find out the starting-point of the action of the drug in the organism. Where and how does the action of the drug first commence? It is the solemn business of pharmacodynamics to acquaint us with this important fact. This fact being known, we have made one great step towards a scientific organization of our Materia Medica. The next step would then be to construct the action of the drug in a complete series by means of our pathological experience at the sick-bed. And this experience must lead us to the same result as the proving of the drug; it must lead us to a precise knowledge of the starting-point of the disease, or of the point where the first invasion of the organism by the morbific principle takes place. Whatever drug-action has the same starting-point with the principle of disease in the organism, would, of course, develope the same series of phenomena which constituted the natural disease, and such a drug would, therefore, be the true curative agent in this particular case. I have said before that this series could not be reproduced in our provings without ruining, and perhaps destroying, the organism; but a sufficient number of prominent symptoms should, at all events, be reproduced to show, by unmistakeable signs, both the starting-point of the drug's action and its general correspondence with the character and symptoms of the disease. No drug can effect a cure whose action upon the organism does not start from the same point as the disease, and no Materia Medica can be considered scientifically arranged, where the pharmacodynamic properties of drugs are not arranged and classified with reference to the phenomena of disease. Let me illustrate this theory by means of one or more drugs in our Materia Medica, say Aconite and Mercurius. In order to determine to what diseases Aconite specifically corresponds as a remedial agent, our first duty is to prove it upon the healthy organism in such a manner as will make us correctly acquainted with the starting-point of its action. We know from a variety of experiments upon men and animals, that the first action of Aconite in the living organism is upon the ganglionic and the capillary systems of nerves. The character of this action is depressing, benumbing, paralysing. Under the influence of Aconite, the pulse gradually sinks until a perfect collapse takes place; the skin becomes cold, the blood seems to retreat from the surface, and the heart's action becomes embarrassed in consequence, which gives rise to depression of spirits, and a state of mental apprehensions, sad forebodings, fitfulness of mood, which is sometimes characterised by the most opposite extremes, such as immoderate, spasmodic laughter, and a moaning and weeping despondency. Without extending this picture of the effects of Aconite upon the organism, it is sufficient for my present purpose to point out the fundamental characteristic of its action, which consists in its depressing effects upon the ganglionic and capillary systems of nerves. From the capillary nerves the effect is necessarily transmitted to the capillary vessels, both arterial and venous, and the first symptom of embarrassment in the capillary circulation is a sense of coldness, shivering, a chill. If the quantity of Aconite, which produced these symptoms, was but small, the natural reaction of the organism will soon overcome the depressing effects of the poison, and an opposite state will develope itself characterised by a full and bounding pulse, warmth of the skin, perspiration. In an actual case of poisoning, the natural reaction of the organism, after the material poison had been withdrawn by means of the stomach-pump or an emetic, may have to be assisted by large quantities of strong coffee, and will then exhibit so much more fully a series of febrile phenomena, or phenomena of venous and arterial congestion.

It being ascertained, by what door, as it were, and in what manner the Aconite-poison invades the organism, our second duty, then, is to determine what disease or diseases, have a similar starting-point as the poison. And we are at once led to that whole class of diseases which are characterized by inflammation and congestion. Aconite, therefore, corresponds specifically with every disease which is characterized by true venous congestion, or synochal inflammation; and, for this reason, it corresponds with all diseases which are legitimate developments of true states of venous congestion or of inflammation, and only differ quantitatively, not qualitatively, in other words, in extent, but not in degree, from the original malady. The suppurative process differs from simple inflammation only in quantity, not quality. An abscess of the liver or psoas-muscle, is the same in degree, but not in extent, as the simple inflammatory condition out of which the abscess had originally developed itself by a process of simple continuation, but not by any essential change of state. Hence, the treatment for both these apparently different conditions, should be the same. If the specific remedy should have been employed for a simple inflammatory tumor, and the suppurative process should nevertheless, develope itself in the course of the treatment, this process will have to be considered, and really is, a curative termination, which, with proper care, and with the use of the ordinary appliances of a poultice, will result in a restoration of the parts. The use of Aconite, in this case, as a positive, specific, remedial agent, does not, by any means, depend upon the exact reproduction, by provings upon the healthy, of all the pains, pathological changes of tissues, etc., which belong to the whole series of morbid phenomena that constitute the disease to be cured. So soon as we are sure that the starting-point of both the drug-action and the action of the morbific principle is the same, we may safely infer that these two forces will correspond throughout the whole line or series of the sensations and changes which characterize their respective action in the living organism. This point being well established, we have acquired the basis of a certain, positive, scientific system of therapeutics, and we have it in our power to apply, with perfect certainty, a certain remedy to morbid phenomena, which may never have been observed by a prover, but which we know form the elements of a series of phenomena that have uniformly, and in accordance with the fixed and immutable laws of physiological and pathological science, developed themselves out of the starting-point which we have been enabled to assign to them. It is, in this way that, knowing as we do, from the beautiful investigations and discoveries of modern science, that all true inflammation and congestion emanates from a depressed, torpid, embarrassed condition of the capillary system of nerves, and knowing, on the other hand, from our provings and from accidental cases of poisoning, that Aconite affects the capillary system in a like manner, which cannot be said of any other known drug: we are authorized to draw this truly saving and glorious conclusion, that Aconite is the specific remedy in all cases of venoso-arterial inflammation and congestion, no matter in what organ or tissue of the organism, the disease may be located. And what is said of Aconite, applies to Mercury and any other drug.

Knowing as we do from experience, that Mercury has the same effect upon the glandular and mucous systems that Aconite has upon the capillary system of nerves, we may conclude, with positive certainty, that this agent will cure every disease which developes itself directly from a depressed, torpid, or embarrassed condition of these respective systems. Even organic diseases, suppurations, indurations, tumours, and enlargements become accessible to treatment in the light of this principle; for, physiology and pathology teach us to trace these disorganizations to their first beginnings, and, in this way, to determine the remedial agent, the action of which, as a crude drug, has the same starting point in the healthy organism, and which is, therefore, alone capable of exercising a retro-formative influence upon the organic disease. Physiology and pathology, which had been excommunicated by

Hahnemann as fallacious speculations, are reinstated as the true bonds of union between pharmacodynamics and therapeutics; a homœopathic physician need no longer suffer himself to be classed among the ignorant charlatans of the day; without the most accurate knowledge of physiology and pathology, it would be impossible for any physician to trace the phenomena of disease to their incipient point, where the organism first became invaded by the morbific principle, and yet, unless this starting-point were exactly known, all rational, that is all certain, positive and specific treatment of disease would be impossible, all true and just criticism of erroneous methods of treatment would be out of the question, all satisfactory explanation of the phenomena of life would remain inaccessible even to the most enlightened understanding, and medicine would remain hereafter, what it has, in a great measure, been heretofore, a system of speculative theories and hypothetical assumptions. A correct knowledge of the physiological functions leads us not only to a precise knowledge of the pathological changes in disease, and informs us, for instance, of the true character of dysentery or piles, whether the disease is a congestion of the mucous coat, or a venoso-arterial congestion of the tissues; this knowledge likewise sheds rays of light upon phenomena, which otherwise could not be adequately combated by specific means. Take, for instance, the phenomena which characterize a state of common synochal fever. We have a full, hard and bounding pulse, a dry and hot skin, moreor less copious perspiration, thirst; all these interesting phenomena can be accounted for in the light of physiology, and, indeed, ought to be accounted for, in order that, on the one hand, we may be enabled to determine the correctness or incorrectness of the treatment of this condition by depletion, and that, on the other hand, we may be guided in an attempt to substitute a true treatment of fever for whatever may have been found to be fallacious in the existing method. Formerly it was supposed that, during a paroxysm of febrile heat, the system makes a good deal more blood than it did immediately previous to the paroxysm, and that, on this account, the volume of blood must be diminished, and the system reduced. This increase of the volume of blood was inferred from the bounding, the fulness and undue strength of the pulse. But a more enlightened knowledge of the physiology of the circulation shows that this notion is erroneous, and that the treatment which is based upon it must be so likewise. How then is the bounding of the pulse to be explained? Is it sufficiently accounted for by setting it down as a sign of reaction? The whole series of phenomena which constitutes, in common parlance, fever, denotes a state of reaction, rather than the original malady; the chill is, properly speaking, the characteristic sign of the primary invasion of the disease. And this fact alone is sufficient to condemn the process of blood-letting as a remedy for fever. For, the chill certainly neither indicates an excess of blood, nor an excited condition of the circulation; on the contrary, the chill is sufficiently accounted for by the fact that the capillary circulation is partially arrested as it were, or embarrassed in consequence of the depression of the capillary nervous action; the oxydation of the tissues is carried on very imperfectly for the time being, and there is, in consequence, a perceptible diminution of animal heat on the cutaneous surfaces. But this condition could not last without leading to a dissolution of the organic tissues. The preservation of the organism renders a reaction against this depressed condition of the vital forces necessary, and this reaction, must, of course, be characterized by the opposite phenomena of a full and bounding pulse, heat and dryness of the skin, thirst, and finally profuse perspiration. The chill having been accounted for, let us now account for the phenomena of reaction, and first of all for the bounding pulse.

The circulatory apparatus may be compared to a balance, composed of the capillary vessels on one side, the larger trunks on the other, and the heart as the pivot or centre. We know that the heart propels the blood through the larger vessels to the terminal capillaries, and that, after having fulfilled the purposes of nutrition, it returns again to the heart from the capillaries through the veins, in an opposite direction. Now, if the route through the capillaries should be stopped or, at any rate, impeded, how will this impediment necessarily affect the larger trunks? The heart propelling the blood with the same or more force and regularity through a shorter channel, the column of blood will necessarily become more agitated in the larger trunks, and these tumultuous movements are characterized by the hardness, quickness and bounding fulness of the pulse. This view of the symptoms shows that the proper means of reducing the pulse, is not an abstraction of blood,—for the quantity of blood is in no way accountable for the altered condition of the pulse,—but a removal of the torpor or embarrassment of the capillary circulation. And this embarrassment depending upon a primary depression of the capillary nerves, it is against this depression that our remedial efforts should be directed. We have seen that Aconite corresponds specifically to such a condition of the capillary nerves, and that it must, on this account, be the specific remedy for fever. And so it is; give the patient a small quantity, say a drop, or even part of a drop of Aconite in a tumblerful of water, and let him drink a portion of this mixture at regular intervals through the day, and the capillary embarrassment will soon yield to the action of the drug, the column of blood will again course with regularity and in perfect freedom through every portion of the circulatory apparatus, and the pulse will become reduced to its normal frequency and strength, without resorting to any of those frightful inroads upon the constitution which often leave the patient debilitated for weeks, months, and even years after the original disease had disappeared. The restoration of the circulation to its original harmony is accompanied by another interesting sign of healthful reaction, the accumulation of moisture upon the cutaneous as well as the inner surfaces, and simultaneously with it the disappearance of the dryness and of the thirst. A correct understanding of this phenomenon will enable us to determine the value of sudorifics in fever for the artificial production of sweat, and we shall have no difficulty in arriving at the important conclusion that there is a great and vital difference between natural sweat and the moisture which sweating medicines, excessive heat, or violent exercise, drive out upon the skin. In the generation and equilibration of the animal heat of the organism, the skin has an important office to perform. It is well known that an essential condition for the generation of animal heat is the oxydation of the tissues. During the chill this oxydation is partially interrupted, and is, on this account, and for the sake of the restoration of the equilibrium, carried on so much the more actively during the process of reaction, or the true inflammatory stage of the fever; hence the buffy coat. I am not, by any means, of the opinion of our chemical physiologists that the oxydation of the tissues is the primary cause of the generation of animal heat; but I look upon it as an essential condition out of which the vital principle evolves the normal temperature of the organism. But the oxydation of the tissues is only one element in the production of animal heat. A counterbalancing influence is required to prevent the evolution of animal heat by the oxydation of the tissues from overstepping its legitimately-conservative boundaries. This counterbalancing influence is the absorption of moisture from the surrounding atmosphere. It is the business of the skin and of the internal mucous surfaces to perform this office, and it is the business of the capillary nerves to enable them to perform it.

I am not aware that this fact has ever been alluded to by chemical physiologists. They talk of the combustion of food in the organism, and of the result of combustion which are carbon and water, but this evidently does not include the natural moisture upon the cutaneous and internal surfaces. For, during the inflammatory stage of the fever, the oxydising process goes on with increased intensity, and yet the skin remains hot and dry. This shows that the natural moisture of the skin must come from some other source, and from what other source could it possibly be derived than from the surrounding atmospheric air? While the capillary system of nerves is embarrassed by some hostile influence, and its action is depressed, the skin and inner surfaces which derive their absorptive power from those nerves, remain dry and hot. But as soon as the embarrassment is removed, the absorption of moisture goes on again with renewed vigor, and in increased quantities, until the temperature of the system is restored to its natural standard. This sweating process is the very opposite of the artificial sweating which is occasioned by the use of sudorific medicines. For, these medicines do not act upon the capillary nerves with a view of relieving them of their embarrassment, and enabling them to resume their functions of absorption by means of the cutaneous organ and the internal mucous surfaces. These medicines act as drains upon the system. All they accomplish is, to drive the vital moisture out upon the skin, which then evaporates and leaves the organism deprived of one of its most essential means of support and restoration. Thirst being occasioned by an interruption of the absorption of moisture from the atmospheric air, it ceases, of course, as soon as this process of absorption is restored in its integrity.

The office, which is performed by the skin and mucous membrane, of absorbing moisture from the atmospheric air, accounts for the fact why fever-patients desire to lie in a cool rather than in a warm room. The air in a cool room contains more moisture than warm air, and, therefore, offers a larger supply to the absorbing surfaces. Upon the same principle a patient suffering with a paroxysm of asthma, or attacked with hydrothorax, desires to be fanned or to have the window opened, in order that the largest possible amount of air may be presented to the lungs.

I have deemed it expedient to explain a few of the phenomena of life to satisfy the reader of the absolute necessity of possessing an accurate knowledge and rational understanding of the physiological functions of the organism in order to conduct the treatment of disease to the satisfaction of one's own internal conscience. Without the aid of physiology and pathology it is useless to attempt to construct the art of healing upon a scientific basis. These twin-sisters of medicine enable us to give a positive direction to our provings towards the sublime object of our art, which is the restoration of health; they enable us to understand the exact meaning, and to measure the true value of our drug-symptoms, and to connect them with the phenomena of disease in such a manner that they shall complete and explain each other, and, by this harmonious alliance, lead us to discover and establish this great and fundamental truth, that a mere apparent similarity of the drug-symptoms and the symptoms of the disease is not sufficient to constitute a certain drug the true remedial agent in a given case; that this similarity is even unnecessary, nay, impossible in many cases; that it is frequently deceptive, almost always incomplete, and that, on this account, the law of cure, as expressed by Hahnemann, although embodying an abstract perception of the truth, is nevertheless a fallacy of the sensual understanding, and not, by any means, a conception of the living reason. And they furthermore teach us, that a drug, in order to acquire the character of a remedial agent in a given case of illness, must invade the organism by the same door, as it were, as the morbific principle. The starting-point of the action of the drug, and that of the disease, must be identical. Then, and only then, is the drug a specific remedial agent in the case, and will effect a speedy, safe and positive cure, provided a cure be at all possible.

And having offered these recapitulations of the general principles which I have endeavored to develope, I will simply ask my readers once more to dwell with particular attention upon the important truth, that the specifically curative character of a drug depends upon the identity of the starting-point of its action upon the organism with the point of invasion of the morbific principle. If these points be identical, the whole action of the drug will correspond with the nature of the disease; not otherwise, be the perceptible symptoms ever so similar. If the true formula of the specific law of cure be then "*Similia similibus,*" this formula should not be understood as simply refering to an outward similarity of the drug-symptoms to the symptoms of the natural disease. This similarity should be understood in a compound sense, as applying to the drug-disease reflected by its pathogenetic symptoms, and to the morbid condition of the organism, or the pathological state, as manifested to the senses by its characteristic phenomena. The formula should, therefore, imply a perfect CORRESPONDENCE between the drug-disease and the natural pathological disturbance as MORBID STATES, not as mere SERIES OF SYMPTOMS, and in order to leave no doubt that this compound similarity or perfect correspondence is the import of the formula, a more adequate expression thereof would be "CORRESPONDENTIA CORRESPONDENTIBUS CURANTUR."

And now, if the remedial character of a drug

depend upon the identity of a mere point, and if, according to the definition of mathematicians, a point be so transcendently delicate, that it is without all space, without all length, breadth, height, or depth, a mere form of thought, instead of a geometrical body, does not then my theory of cure, if the mode of reasoning which I have adopted, be otherwise correct,—and I humbly submit that it is,—naturally lead to a justification of the small doses of medicine which homœopathic physicians generally use in their practice? If the cure of a disease depend upon the identity of its point of invasion with the starting-point of the drug-action, then the disease itself, so far as the therapeutic process is concerned, is undoubtedly reduced to a mere point, and that point not even a concrete body, but such an immaterial something, that it seems more like a mere form of thought, a spiritual perception, than a palpable substance. And it would seem as though to combat a mere point, could not possibly require massive doses of the crude drug. And even, if we admit, that the reduction of the dose ought to have its limits in the present condition of our sensual existence, and that, beyond these limits, all further reduction becomes a senseless waste of time and an imposition upon the credulity of our patients, it would seem, on the other hand, providing my mode of reasoning is correct, that the smallness of the doses which homœopathic physicians have been in the habit of using, has a legitimate claim to the respectful regard of true science, and that such doses can no longer appear ridiculous before the tribunal of enlightened practitioners. Theoretically, the dose may be a mere point; practically, it may be one or more grains of the prepared drug, a drop or two of the tincture, or part of a drop; and, under certain circumstances, this part may even be infinitesimally small. A vast quantity of bitter and profitless controversies have been carried on concerning the true size of homœopathic doses; and the question is still as far from being settled as ever. The determination of the suitable dose in a case depends, for the present at least, upon the skill and judgment of the individual physician. One of the great reasons why the dose was gradually reduced by Hahnemann to the infinitesimal portion of a drop, was the idea he entertained, that a larger dose would produce an aggravation of the symptoms of the disease. The doctrine of aggravations became a settled doctrine in homœopathic practice, and it was finally supposed that no cure could be effected according to the homœopathic law, without a previous aggravation of the symptoms. But this whole theory of aggravations must be set down as a metaphysical subtlety, which has little, if any, foundation in actual observation. Aggravations have undoubtedly occurred, and do occur, after the exhibition of a homœopathic agent; but such aggravations are scarcely ever attributable to the action of the drug, but constitute a natural development of the disease, owing probably to the inefficiency of the dose or of the medicine employed. Both patients and physicians are too much in the habit of attributing any unfavorable changes, that may occur in the symptoms of the disease, after the exhibition of a certain drug, to the agency of this medicine. This is, generally speaking, a mistake, which gives rise to a great many important and even dangerous errors in practice. In prescribing specific remedies, it is, of course, advisable to begin with the smallest possible dose, but it is unnecessary to be frightened, at every nook and corner of the treatment, by the bugbear of medicinal aggravations.

My work is ended. To some it may prove acceptable, to others objectionable. I have endeavored to be just, although the interests of true science have at times obliged me to use the pruning-knife of criticism without friendship or favor. Truth never loses by candor, and doctrines which do not bear a critical examination, have no business to claim our respect on the score of expediency or traditional authority. Let us then continue to prove all things, until truth shall have descended amongst us in all the glory of her divine lineage, and every man shall have become what the Creator originally designed he should be, a living form of love and wisdom.

THE END.

INDEX.

PART I.

PART II.

PART III.

ERRATA.

Page 107, line 2 from below, instead of "changed," read "chained."
" 154, " 14 " " leave out "not."

New Manual of Homœopathic Veterinary Medicine, an easy and comprehensive arrangement of Diseases, and adapted to the use of every owner of Domestic Animals, but especially of the farmer living out of the reach of medical advice, and showing him the way of treating his sick Horses, Cattle, Sheep, Swine and Dogs, in the most simple, expeditious, safe and cheap manner. By J. E. Schæfer. Translated from the German. With numerous additions, by W. H. Smith, Veterinary Surgeon of this City.

Schæfer's New Manual will be issued on the 1st of July, 1854.

A.

A Concise View of the System of Homœopathy, and Refutation of the Objections commonly brought forward against it. Dublin, 1845. Stitched $1 00.

Address delivered before the American Institute of Homœopathy at its annual meeting in Albany in 1850, with an account of the Proceedings. By A. E. Small, M. D., Professor of Physiology and Pathology. 25 cents.

Address delivered to the Homœopathic Medical College of Pennsylvania as a Preliminary to the Course of 1849–1850. By A. E. Small, M. D., Professor of Physiology and Pathology. 13 cents.

Atkin, Dr. George. The British and Foreign Homœopathic Medical Directory and Record. Issued July 1, 1853. London. Bound $1 50.

B.

Becker, Dr. A. C., On Constipation. Translated from the German, 1848. Bound, 38 cents.

Becker, Dr. A. C., On Consumption. Translated from the German. 1848. Bound, 38 cents.

Becker, Dr. A. C., On Dentition. Translated from the German. 1848. Bound, 38 cents.

Becker, Dr. A. C., On Diseases of the Eye. Translated from the German. 1848. Bound, 38 cents.

☞ The above four works by Dr. A. C. Becker, can be had bound in one volume, at $1 00.

Bœnninghausen's Essay on the Homœopathic Treatment of Intermittent Fevers. Translated and Edited by C. J. Hempel, M. D. 1845. 38 cts.

Bryant, Dr. J., A Pocket Manual or Repertory of Homœopathic Medicine, alphabetically and nosologically arranged; which may be used as the physician's Vade-Mecum, the traveller's Medical Companion, or the Family Physician: containing the principal remedies for the most important diseases, symptoms, sensations, characteristics of diseases, &c.; with the principal pathogenetic effects of the medicines on the most important organs and functions of the body; together with diagnosis, explanation of technical terms, directions for the selection and exhibition of remedies, rules of diet, &c., &c. Compiled from the best homœopathic authorities. 1851. Bound, $1 25.

C.

Calman, Dr. Ludwig, Homœopathy the True Healing Art. London. Paper cover, 38 cents.

Caspari's Homœopathic Domestic Physician, edited by F. Hartmann, M. D., "Author of the Acute and Chronic Diseases." Translated from the eighth German edition, and enriched by a Treatise on Anatomy and Physiology, embellished with 30 illustrations by W. P. Esrey, M. D. With additions and a preface by C. Hering, M. D. Containing also a chapter on Mesmerism and Magnetism; directions for patients living some distance from a homœopathic physician, to describe their symptoms; a Tabular

Index of the medicines and the diseases in which they are used; and a Sketch of the Biography of Dr. Samuel Hahnemann, the Founder of Homœopathy. 1851. Bound, $1 25.

Chepmell, Dr. E. C., Domestic Homœopathy restricted to its legitimate sphere of practice, together with rules for diet and regimen. First American edition, with additions and improvements by Samuel B. Barlow, M. D. 1849. Bound, 50 cents.

Croserio, Dr. C., Homœopathic Manual of Obstetrics: or a Treatise on the aid the art of Midwifery may derive from Homœopathy. From the French by M. Coté, M. D. 1853. Bound, 75 cents.

D.

Defence of Hahnemann and his Doctrines, including an exposure of Dr. Alex. Wood's "Homœopathy Unmasked." London, 1844. 50 cts.

Dysentery and its Homœopathic Treatment. Containing also a Repertory and numerous Cases, by Fred. Humphreys, M. D., Professor of Homœopathic Institutes, Pathology and the Practice of Medicine in the Homœopathic Medical College of Pennsylvania. 1853. Bound, 50 cents.

E.

Elements of Veterinary Homœopathy, embracing hints on the Application of Hydropathy: or a Treatise on the Diseases of the Horse and Cow; with remarks on the general Management and principal Diseases incidental to the Sheep and Dog. By W. Haycock, V. S., Member of the Veterinary College, Edinburgh. London, 1852. Bound, $3 50.

Epitome of Homœopathic Practice. Compiled chiefly from Jahr, Rückert, Beauvais, Bœnninghausen, &c. By J. T. Curtis, M. D., and J. Lillie, M. D. Second enlarged edition. 1850. Bound, 75 cents.

Epps, Dr. J., Affections of the Head and the nervous System. London. Bound, $1 00.

Epps, Dr. J., Domestic Homœopathy; or Rules for the Domestic Treatment of the Maladies of Infants, Children and Adults, and for the conduct and the treatment during Pregnancy, Confinement, and Suckling. Fifth American, from the Fourth London edition. Edited and enlarged by John A. Tarbell, M. D. 1853. Bound, 75 cents.

Esrey, Dr. W. P., Treatise on Anatomy and Physiology. With 30 illustrations. 195 pages. 1851. Bound, 50 cents.

☞ Dr. W. P. Esrey's Treatise on Anatomy and Physiology, is the cheapest book ever published on those subjects, and is particularly of great use to Students of Medicine as a compendium.

Eustaphieve, A., Homœopathy Revealed. A brief exposition of the whole system, adapted to general comprehension; with a notice of Psora and Dr. Durange's objections. Second edition, with a Sketch of Isopathia. 50 cents.

F.

Flora Homœopathica; or Illustrations and Descriptions of the Medical Plants used as Homœopathic Remedies. By Edward Hamilton, M. D., F. L. S. The work is illustrated by Henry Sowerby, from Drawings made expressly for the Author. The Flora Homœopathica contains a colored illustration and complete history of every plant generally employed in Homœopathic Pharmacy, arranged in alphabetical order. The drawings are chiefly made from natural specimens, and to ensure correctness, the Author has secured the services of Mr. Henry Sowerby, the Assistant Curator of the Linnean Society. With a Preface, Glossary of Botanical terms and Index. London, 1853. Price for the whole work, containing sixty-six handsomely colored plates, elegantly bound. $18 00.

Forbes, Dr. J., Homœopathy, Allopathy, and Young Physic. 1846. Paper cover, 19 cents.

G.

Guenther, Dr. E. A., New Manual of Homœopathic Veterinary Medicine; or the Homœopathic Treatment of the Horse, the Ox, the Sheep, the Dog, and other Domestic Animals. 1847. Bound, $1 25.

Guernsey's Homœopathic Domestic Practice. Containing also Chapters on Anatomy, Physiology, Hygiene, and an Abridged Materia Medica. 1853. Bound, $1 50.

H.

Hahnemann, Dr. Samuel, The Lesser Writings of, collected and translated by R. E. Dudgeon, M. D. With a Preface and Notes by E. E. Marcy, M. D. With a beautiful steel engraving of Hahnemann, from the statue by Steinhæuser. Bound, $3 00.

☞ This valuable work contains a large number of Essays of great interest to laymen as well as medical men, upon diet, the prevention of diseases, ventilation of dwellings, etc. As many of these papers were written before the discovery of the Homœopathic theory of cure, the reader will be enabled to peruse in this volume the ideas of a gigantic intellect when directed to subjects of general and practical interest.

Hahnemann, Dr. Samuel, Materia Medica Pura. Translated by C. J. Hempel, M. D. 4 vols. 1846. Bound, $6.

Hahnemann, Dr. Samuel, the Chronic Diseases, their Specific Nature and Homœopathic Treatment. Translated and edited by C. J. Hempel, M. D., with a Preface by C. Hering, M. D., Philadelphia. 5 vols. 1849. $7. Bound,

Hahnemann, Dr. Samuel, Organon of Homœopathic Medicine, third American edition, with improvements and additions from the last German edition, and Dr. C. Hering's introductory remarks. 1848. Bound, $1.

☞ The above four works of Dr. Samuel Hahnemann, are and will forever be the greatest treasures of Homœopathy; they are the most necessary works for Homœopathic Practitioners, and should grace the library of every Homœopathic Physician.

Hamilton, Dr. Edward, Guide to the Practice of Homœopathy; translated and compiled in alphabetical order, from the German of Ruoff, Haas, and Rueckert. With many additions. London, 1844. Bound, $1 50.

Hartmann, Dr. F., Acute and Chronic Diseases, and their Homœopathic Treatment. Third German edition, revised and considerably enlarged by the author. Translated, with additions, and adapted to the use of the American profession, by C. J. Hempel, M. D. 4 vols. $5 75.

Hartmann, Dr. F., Diseases of Children and their Homœopathic Treatment. Translated, with notes, and prepared for the use of the American and English Profession, by Charles J. Hempel, M. D. 1853. Bound, $2.

Hartmann, Dr. F., Practical Observations on some of the chief Homœopathic Remedies. Translated from the German by A. H. Okie, M. D. Two series. Bound, $2.

Hempel, Dr. Charles Julius, Organon of Specific Homœopathy; or, an Inductive Exposition of the Principles of the Homœopathic Healing Art, addressed to Physicians and intelligent Laymen, by Charles J. Hempel, M. D., Fellow and Corresponding member of the Homœopathic Medical College of Pennsylvania; Honorary Member of the Hahnemann Society of London, &c. &c. Bound, $1.

Hempel, Dr. Charles Julius, A Treatise on the Use of Arnica, in cases of Contusions, Wounds, Sprains, Lacerations of the Solids, Concussions, Paralysis, Rheumatism, Soreness of the Nipples, &c., &c., with a number of cases illustrative of the use of that drug. 1845. 19 cents.

Hempel, Dr. Charles Julius, Complete Repertory of the Homœopathic Materia Medica. Being the Third volume of Jahr's New Manual, or Symptomen-Codex, and the most important and complete work ever published, and indispensable for every Homœopathic Practitioner. 1224 pages. 1853. Bound, $6 00.

Hempel's Bœnninghausen's Therapeutic Pocket Book, for Homœopathic Physicians; to be used at the bedside of the patient, and in studying the Materia Medica Pura. 1 octavo vol., most complete edition, including the Concordance of Homœopathic Remedies. Translated and adapted to the use of the American profession, by C. J. Hempel, M. D. 1847. Stitched, $1 50. Bound, $2 00.

Hempel's Homœopathic Domestic Physician. 1850. Bound, 50 cents.

Henderson, Dr. Wm., Homœopathic Practice. 1846. 50 cents.

Henderson, Dr. Wm., Letter to J. Forbes. 1846. 19 cents.

Hering, Dr. C., Domestic Physician, revised with additions from the author's manuscript of the *Seventh German Edition.* Containing also a Tabular Index of the medicines and the diseases in which they are used. *Fifth American Edition.* 1851. Bound, $2 00.

☞ *Dr. C. Hering's Domestic Physician* is also to be had of the subscribers in *German,* (eighth edition,) *French* (second edition,) and *Spanish.*

Homœopathic Cookery. Second edition, with additions, by the Lady of an American Homœopathic Physician. Designed chiefly for the use of such persons as are under homœopathic treatment. Bound, 50 cents.

Homœopathic Treatment of Diseases of the Sexual System, being a complete Repertory of all the symptoms occurring in the Sexual Systems of the Male and Female. Adapted to the use of physicians and laymen. Translated, arranged and edited, with additions and improvements, by Dr. F. Humphreys. Second thousand, 1854. Bound, 50 cents.

Hooker, Dr. Worthington, Homœopathy: An Examination of its Doctrines and Evidences. Second edition, 1852. Bound, $1 50.

Humphreys, Dr. F., the Cholera and its Homœopathic Treatment. 1849. Bound, 38 cents.

Hydriatics; or Manual of the Water Cure, especially as practised by Vincent Priessnitz in Graefenberg. Compiled and translated from the writings of Dr. Charles Munde, Dr. Aertel, Dr. B. Hirschel, and other eye-witnesses and practitioners. By Francis Græter. 1843. Bound, 50 cts.

J.

Jahr, Dr. G. H. G., Clinical Guide, or Pocket-Repertory for the Treatment of Acute and Chronic Diseases. Translated from the German, by C. J. Hempel, M. D. 1850. Bound, $1 50.

Jahr, Dr. G. H. G., Diseases of the Skin; or Alphabetical Repertory of the Skin-symptoms and external alterations of substance, together with the morbid phenomena observed in the glandular, osseous, mucous, and circulatory systems, arranged with pathological remarks on the diseases of the skin. Edited by C. J. Hempel, M. D. 1850. Bound, $1.

Jahr, Dr. G. H. G., and **Gruner's** New Homœopathic Pharmacopœia and Posology, or the Mode of Preparing Homœopathic Medicine, and the Administration of Doses, compiled and translated from the German works of Buchner, Gruner, and the French work of Jahr, by C. J. Hempel, M. D., 1850. Bound, $2.

Jahr, Dr. G. H. G., and **Possart's** New Manual of the Homœopathic Materia Medica, arranged with reference to well authenticated observations at the sick bed, and accompanied by an alphabetical Repertory, to facilitate and secure the selection of a suitable remedy in any given case. Fourth edition, revised and enlarged by the Author, and translated and edited by Charles J. Hempel, M. D., 1853. Bound, $3 50.

Jahr, Dr. G. H. G., New Manual: originally published under the name of Symptomen-Codex (Digest of Symptoms). This work is intended to facilitate a comparison of the parallel symptoms of the various Homœopathic agents, thereby enabling the practitioner to discover the characteristic symptoms of each drug, and to determine with ease and correctness what remedy is most homœopathic to the existing group of symptoms.

Translated, with important and extensive additions from various sources, by Charles Julius Hempel, M. D., assisted by James M. Quin, M. D., with revisions and clinical notes by John F. Gray, M. D.; contributions by Drs. A. Gerald Hull, George W. Cook, and B. F. Joslin of New York; and Drs. C. Hering, J. Jeanes, C. Neidhard, W. Williamson, and J. Kitchen of Phila.; with a Preface by C. Hering, M. D. 2 vols., 1848. Bound, $11.

☞ **Jahr's** New Manual or Symptomen Codex, is published in three volumes, of which the third was issued as a separate work, under the title of Complete Repertory of the Homœopathic Materia Medica. By Charles J. Hempel, M. D., 1224 pages. Price $6 00, or all 3 volumes at $17 00.

Jahr, Dr. G. H. G., New Manual of Homœopathic Practice; edited, with Annotations, by A. Gerald Hull, M. D. From the last Paris edition. This is the fourth American edition of a very celebrated work, written in French by the eminent homœopathic Professor Jahr, and it is considered the best practical compendium of this extraordinary science that has yet been composed. After a very judicious and instructive introduction, the work presents a Table of the Homœopathic Medicines, with their names in Latin, English and German; the order in which they are to be studied, with their most important distinctions, and clinical illustrations of their symptoms and effects upon the various organs and functions of the human system. The second volume embraces an elaborate Analysis of the indications in disease, of the medicines adapted to cure, and a Glossary of the technics used in the work, arranged so luminously as to form an admirable guide to every medical student. The whole system is here displayed with a modesty of pretension, and a scrupulosity in statement, well calculated to bespeak candid investigation. This laborious work is indispensable to the students and practitioners of homœopathy, and highly interesting to medical scientific men of all classes. 2 vols., 1850. $6.

Joslin, Dr. B. F., Homœopathic Treatment of Diarrhœa, Dysentery, Cholera Morbus, and Cholera, with repertory. Bound, 50 cents.

Joslin, Dr. B. F., Principles of Homœopathia. In a series of lectures. 1850. Bound, 75 cents.

L.

Laurie's Homœopathic Domestic, by A. Gerald Hull, M. D. Small edition. 1848. Bound, 75 cents.

Laurie, Dr. J., Elements of Homœopathic Practice of Physic. Second American edition, enlarged and improved, by A. Gerald Hull, M. D., and an Appendix on Intermittent Fever, by J. S. Douglas, A. M., M. D. 1853. 939 large 8vo. pages. Bound, $3 00.

Laurie, Dr. J., Elements of Homœopathic Practice of Physic. An Appendix to Laurie's Domestic, containing also all the Diseases of the *Urinary and Genital Organs.* 1849. Bound, $1 25.

Laurie's Homœopathic Domestic Medicine. Arranged as a practical work for Students. Containing a Glossary of medical terms. Sixth American edition, enlarged and improved, by A. Gerald Hull, M. D. 1853. Bound, $2 00.

Law of Cure. Dr. Joslin's Address before the American Institute of Homœopathy, held at Philadelphia, June 13, 1850. 13 cents.

☞ To physicians wishing the Law of Cure for distribution, we will sell 12 copies for $1.

Lazarus, Dr. M. E., Homœopathy, a Theoretic Demonstration with social Applications. 1851. Bound, 37½ cents.

Lazarus, Dr. M. E., Involuntary Seminal Losses: their Causes, Effects and Cure. 1852. Paper cover, 25 cents.

M.

Madden's Uterine Diseases, with an Appendix containing abstracts of 180 Cases of Uterine Diseases and their Treatment, together with Analytical Tables of Results, Ages, Symptoms, Dose, etc., to which is added a Clinical Record of interesting cases treated in the Manchester Homœopathic Hospital. 1852. Paper cover, 50 cents.

Malan's Family Guide to the Administration of Homœopathic Remedies. Bound, 25 cts.

Marcy, Dr. E. E., Homœopathy and Allœopathy; Reply to an Examination of the Doctrines and Evidences of Homœopathy, by Worthington Hooker, M. D. 1853. Bound, 50 cents.

Marcy, Dr. E. E., the Homœopathic Theory and Practice of Medicine. 1850. Bound, $2.

Mariner's Physician and Surgeon; or, a Guide to the Homœopathic Treatment of those diseases to which Seamen are liable. By Geo. W. Cook, M. D. 1848. Bound, 37½ cents.

Materia Medica of American Provings. By C. Hering, M. D., J. Jeanes, M. D., C. B. Matthews, M. D., W. Williamson, M. D., C. Neidhard, M. D., S. R. Dubs, M. D., C. Bute, M. D. Containing the Provings of: Acidum benzoicum, Acidum fluoricum, Acidum oxalicum, Elaterium, Eupatorium perfoliatum, Kalmia latifolia, Lobelia inflata, Lobelia cardinalis, Podophyllum peltatum, Sanguinaria canadensis and Triosteum perfoliatum. Collected and arranged by the American Institute of Homœopathy. With a Repertory by W. P. Esrey, M. D. Second Thousand. 1853. Bound, $1.

N.

Neidhard, Dr. Charles, Homœopathy in Germany and England in 1849, with a glance at Allœopathic men and things. Being two preliminary discourses, delivered in the Homœopathic Medical College of Pennsylvania. 13 cents.

P.

Peters, Dr. John C., A Treatise on the Diseases of Females. Disorders of Menstruation. 1853. Bound, 75 cents.

Pocket-Homœopathist, and Family Guide. By J. A. Tarbell, M. D. 1849. Bound, 25 cents.

Provings of the Apis Mellifica, or Poison of the Honey Bee. By Drs. Bishop, Humphreys and Munger. 1852. Paper cover, 25 cents.

Pulte's Homœopathic Domestic Physician, containing the Treatment of Diseases; with popular explanations of Anatomy, Physiology, Hygiene and Hydropathy; also an abridged Materia Medica. Illustrated with anatomical plates. Fourth edition. 1853. Bound, $1 50.

Pulte's Woman's Medical Guide; containing Essays on the Physical, Moral and Educational development of Females, and the Homœopathic Treatment of their diseases in all periods of Life, together with Directions for the Remedial use of Water and Gymnastics. 1853. Bound, $1 00.

R.

Reason why Homœopathy should receive an Impartial Investigation from the Medical Profession and the Public. By B. F. Bowers, M. D., 18 cents.

Rapou, Dr. Aug., Treatise on Typhoid Fever, and its Homœopathic Treatment. Translated from the French, by Arthur Alleyn Granville. 1853. Bound, 50 cents.

Rau, Dr. G. L., Organon of the Specific Healing Art of Homœopathy, by C. J. Hempel, M. D. Bound, $1 25.

Report of the Edinburgh Homœopathic Dispensary for 1841–1842. 38 cents.

Rueckert, Dr. Th. J., Apoplexy and Palsy. Successful Homœopathic cures, collected from the best homœopathic periodicals. Translated and edited by J. C. Peters, M. D. With full descriptions of the dose to each single case. 1853. Bound, 75 cents.

Rueckert, Dr. Th. J., Diseases of the Eye and Ear. Successful homœopathic cures, collected from the best homœopathic periodicals. Translated and edited by J. C. Peters, M. D. With full descriptions of the dose to each single case. 1854. Bound, 75 cents.

Rueckert, Dr. Th. J., Diseases of the Stomach. Successful Homœopathic cures, collected from the best homœopathic periodicals. Translated and edited by J. C. Peters, M. D. With full descriptions of the dose to each single case. 1854. Bound, 75 cents.

Rueckert, Dr. Th. J., Inflammation and Dropsy of the Brain. Successful Homœopathic cures, collected from the best homœopathic periodicals. Translated and edited by J. C. Peters, M. D. With full descriptions of the dose to each single case. 1854. Bound, 75 cents.

Rueckert, Dr. Th. J., Nervous Diseases and Mental Derangements. Successful Homœopathic cures, collected from the best homœopathic periodicals. Translated and edited by J. C. Peters, M. D. With full descriptions of the dose to each single case. 1854. Bound, 75 cents.

Rueckert, Dr. Th. J., Treatise on Headaches; including acute, chronic, nervous, gastric, dyspeptic or sick headaches; also congestive, rheumatic and periodical headaches. Based on clinical experience in Homœopathy. With Introduction, Appendix, Synopsis, Notes, Directions for doses, and 50 additional cases, by John C. Peters, M. D., 1853. Bound, 75 cents.

Rueckert, Dr. Ernest Ferdinand, Therapeutics; or, Successful Homœopathic cures, collected from the best homœopathic periodicals. Translated and edited by C. J. Hempel, M. D. 1 large 8vo. vol. 1846. Bound, $3 50.

Ruoff's Repertory of Homœopathic Medicine, nosologically arranged. Translated from the German by A. H. Okie, M. D., translator of Hartmann's Remedies. Second American edition, with additions and improvements, by G. Humphrey, M. D. 1845. Bound, $1 50.

Simpson, Professor Dr. James Y., Homœopathy: its Tenets and Tendencies, theoretical, theological, and therapeutical. Third edition. Edinburgh, 1853. Bound, $2 25.

Stapf, Dr. E., Addition to the Materia Medica Pura. Translated by C. J. Hempel, M. D. Bound, $1 50.

Tarbell, Dr. J. A., Sources of Health, and the Prevention of Disease. 1850. Bound, 50 cts.

Vanderburgh, Dr. F., an Appeal for Homœopathy; or, Remarks on the Decision of the late Judge Cowan, relative to the legal rights of homœopathic physicians. 1844. 13 cents.

HOMŒOPATHIC JOURNALS.

The Philadelphia Journal of Homœopathy. Edited by William A. Gardiner, M. D., Professor of Anatomy in the Homœopathic Medical College of Pennsylvania, assisted by the following contributors: Drs. B. F. Joslin, A. H. Okie, H. C. Preston, J. P. Dake, P. P. Wells, W. E. Payne. C. Dunham, James Kitchen, W. S. Helmuth, A. E. Small, S. R. Dubs, W. E. Payne. Published Monthly by Rademacher & Sheek, 239 Arch st., Phila. Price per volume of 12 monthly numbers, free of postage, $3 00.

The North American Homœopathic Journal, a quarterly Magazine of Medicine and the Auxiliary Sciences. Conducted by C. Hering, M. D., Philadelphia; E. E. Marcy, M. D., and J. W. Metcalf, M. D., New York. Price per volume of 586 octavo pages, $3.

The British Journal of Homœopathy, edited by J. J. Drysdale, M. D., J. R. Russell, M. D., and R. J. Dudgeon, M. D. Price per volume, $3 00. The numbers of 1849, 1850, 1851, 1852 and 1853, are on hand, at $3 each vol. of four quarterly numbers, with title and index.

The Homœopathic Examiner, Vols. I. and II., new series, by Drs. Gray and Hempel, 1845–1847. Bound, in two vols., with an inoptical index of the two vols., to be used as a manual. $5 00.

Boston Quarterly Homœopathic Journal. Edited by Drs. Joseph Birnstill and B. de Gersdorf. Vol. I., 1849, Vol. II., 1850. Price per Vol. in numbers, $3, bound per Vol., $3 50.

Quarterly Homœopathic Journal. Edited by Drs. J. Birnstill and J. A. Tarbell. Boston. Price per year, $1 00.

www.ingramcontent.com/pod-product-compliance
Lightning Source LLC
LaVergne TN
LVHW050530100826
845148LV00002B/506
* 9 7 8 1 4 2 5 5 1 9 2 6 1 *